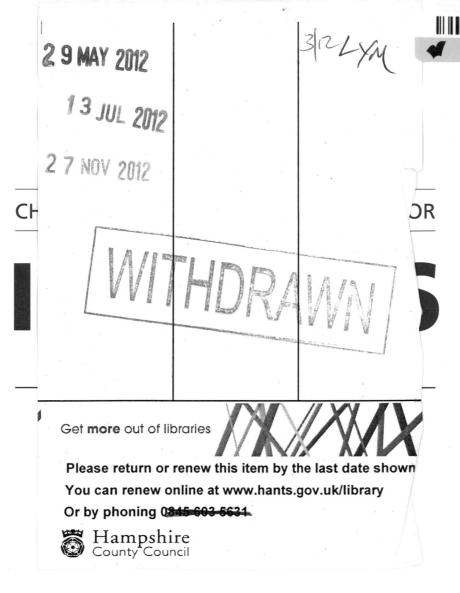

CH...OR

Rawdon Wyatt

First published in Great Britain 2001 by A & C Black Publishers Ltd

This second edition published 2012 by

Bloomsbury Publishing Plc
50 Bedford Square
London
WC1B 3DP
www.bloomsbury.com

A CIP record for this book is available from the British Library.

ISBN: 978-1-4081-5393-2

This book is produced using paper that is made from wood grown in
managed, sustainable forests. It is natural, renewable and recyclable.
The logging and manufacturing processes conform to the
environmental regulations of the country of origin.

Typeset by Saxon Graphics Ltd, Derby
Printed and bound in Great Britain by MPG Books Limited

About this workbook

Introduction

This workbook has been written for students who are planning to sit either the Academic or General Training modules of the IELTS examination. It covers some of the main vocabulary areas that you will need for, or come across in, the Listening, Reading, Writing and Speaking sections of the exam.

We hope that you find the exercises in this book useful, and that the vocabulary you acquire will help you to achieve the grade you want in the IELTS.

Good luck!

Structure of the book

Each vocabulary area is presented in the form of a self-contained module with task-based activities which present each vocabulary item in context.

- Pages 1 – 57 focus on general vocabulary items. Some of these are relevant to specific tasks or questions in the IELTS examination (for example, describing how something works, talking about changes shown in a graph or table, saying where things are and following directions).

- Pages 58 – 104 focus on topic-specific vocabulary areas which may be required in the examination (for example, education, architecture, family matters and science and technology). Each module consists of three tasks: the first two present vocabulary items in context, each with a practice or recognition exercise, and the third gives you the opportunity to review the vocabulary in a gap-fill exercise.

- Pages 105 – 124 contain a comprehensive key so you can check your answers. The answer key also gives additional information about specific vocabulary items or general vocabulary areas, as well as other useful words or phrases.

Using the workbook

You should not work through the book mechanically from beginning to end. It is better to choose areas that you are unfamiliar with, or areas that you feel are of specific interest or importance to yourself.

Recording, reviewing and extending your vocabulary

Remember that you should keep a record of new words, phrases and expressions that you acquire, and review these on a regular basis so that they become part of your active vocabulary. Also remember that there are other ways of acquiring new vocabulary. For example, you should read as much as possible from a variety of authentic reading materials (books, newspapers, magazines, web-based articles, etc.).

Using an English dictionary

To help you develop your vocabulary more effectively, you should use a good monolingual English dictionary. This should clearly explain what the words mean, show you how they are pronounced, show you their various forms where relevant (e.g., what the noun form of an adjective is), tell you which words or phrases they collocate with, and give sample sentences to show you how the words are used. We particularly recommend the *Macmillan English Dictionary for Advanced Learners* (ISBN 978-1405026284). A free on-line version of this can also be found at www.macmillandictionary.com.

The International English Language Testing System (IELTS)

The IELTS is administered by the University of Cambridge Local Examinations Syndicate (UCLES), the British Council and IDP Education Australia. For further information, visit www.ucles.org.uk. Note that this book is not endorsed by any of these organisations.

Contents

Addition, equation & conclusion

1 Put the following words and phrases into their correct place in the table depending on their function.

> along with   also   ~~and~~   as well as   besides   correspondingly
> ~~equally~~   furthermore   in addition   in brief   ~~in conclusion~~
> in the same way   likewise   moreover   similarly   thus   therefore
> to conclude   to summarise   to sum up briefly   too
> we can conclude that   what's more

Addition	Equation	Conclusion
and	equally	in conclusion

2 Complete these sentences with one of the words or phrases from above. In most cases, more than one answer is possible.

1. Tourism brings much-needed money to developing countries. .... , it provides employment for the local population.

2. .... bringing much-needed money to developing countries, tourism provides employment for the local population.

3. Tourists should respect the local environment. .... they should respect the local customs.

4. .... industrial waste, pollution from car fumes is poisoning the environment.

5. In order to travel, you need a passport. .... , you might need a visa, immunisation jabs and written permission to visit certain areas.

6. Drugs are banned in Britain - .... weapons such as guns and knives.

7. All power corrupts. .... , absolute power corrupts absolutely.

8. You shouldn't smoke, drink, take drugs or eat unhealthy food. .... , you should live a more healthy lifestyle.

9. The ozone layer is becoming depleted, the air in the cities is becoming too dirty to breathe and our seas and rivers are no longer safe to swim in. .... pollution is slowly destroying the planet.

10. Your grades have been very poor for the past two years. .... you need to work really hard if you want to pass your exams next month.

Around the world

1 Choose the correct word or phrase in bold to complete these sentences.

1. Japan, Korea and Taiwan are all in **the Near East / the Middle East / the Far East**.

2. The South Pole is situated in the **Arctic / Antarctic / Antarctica**.

3. New Zealand is part of **Austria / Australia / Australasia**.

4. Bangladesh is part of **the Indian subcontinent / India / Indiana**.

5. Guatemala is a country in **North America / South America / Central America**.

6. Argentina, Brazil, Colombia, Panama and Honduras all form part of what is often referred to as **Latin America / South America / Spanish America**.

7. Botswana is in **South Africa / southern Africa / Central Africa**.

8. England, Scotland, Wales and Northern Ireland are known collectively as **Britain / Great Britain / the United Kingdom**.

9. The United Kingdom and the Republic of Ireland are part of **Continental Europe / Mainland Europe / Europe**.

10. Kuwait, Oman and the United Arab Emirates form part of what are known as **the West Indies / the Gulf States / the European Union**.

11. Denmark, Finland, Norway and Sweden are known collectively as **the Baltic Republics / the Caribbean / Scandinavia**.

12. Bangkok, Lima and Tunis are examples of **capital / capitol / capitalism** cities.

2 What are the nationalities of the people who come from these countries?

1. Afghanistan *Afghan*

2. Argentina ....

3. Australia ....

4. Bangladesh ....

5. Belgium....................

6. Brazil....................

7. Canada....................

8. Denmark ....

9. Egypt....................

10. England....................

11. Finland....................

12. Greece....................

13. India ....

14. Iran....................

15. Iraq....................

16. Ireland....................

17. Israel....................

18. Japan....................

19. Kuwait....................

20. Lebanon....................

21. Malaysia....................

22. Mexico....................

23. Morocco....................

24. the Netherlands ....

25. Norway....................

26. Pakistan ....

27. Peru....................

28. the Philippines....................

29. Poland....................

30. Portugal ....

31. Russia ....

32. Saudi Arabia ....

33. Scotland ....

34. Spain ....

35. Sweden ....

36. Switzerland....................

37. Thailand....................

38. Turkey ....

39. Wales ....

40. Yemen....................

Is your country on this list? If not, how do you say your nationality in English? ....

Changes 1

1 Look at the graph, and complete the sentences with the correct form of the words and phrases in the box. In most cases, more than one option is possible.

decline	decrease	drop	fall	fluctuate	go down
go up	~~increase~~	peak at	reach a peak of	remain constant	
remain steady	rise				

English school student numbers: May – August.

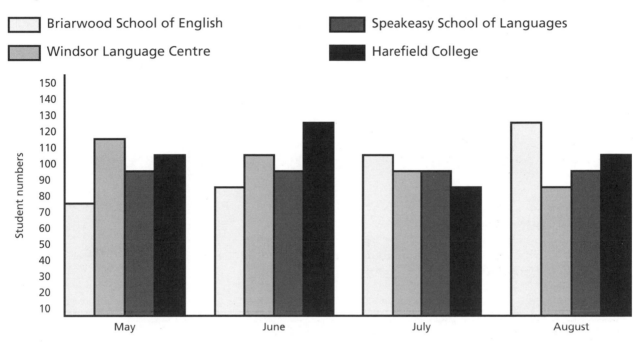

Briarwood School of English   Speakeasy School of Languages
Windsor Language Centre   Harefield College

Between May and August…

1. …student numbers at the Briarwood School of English *increased* / .... / ....

2. …student numbers at the Windsor Language Centre .... / .... / .... /
    .... / ....

3. …student numbers at the Speakeasy School of Languages .... / ....

4. …student numbers at Harefield College .... They .... / .... 120 in June.

2 Look at this table, and complete the sentences on the next page with words and phrases from the box. In some cases, more than one answer is possible. There is one word or phrase that you do not need.

Petrol prices			
January	£1.10 / litre	June	£1.55 / litre
February	£1.12 / litre	July	£1.52 / litre
March	£1.15 / litre	August	£1.53 / litre
April	£1.18 / litre	September	£1.58 / litre
May	£1.16 / litre	October	£1.60 / litre

downward trend	dramatically	gradually	sharply	slightly	steadily
upward trend					

Changes 1

1. Between January and April, petrol prices increased .... / ....

2. In May, petrol prices fell ....

3. In June, petrol prices rose .... / ....

4. Overall, there has been an .... in petrol prices

3 Look at the task in the box, then complete the sample answer with words and phrases from Exercises 1 and 2. In some cases, more than one answer may be possible.

> *The graph below shows the number of visitors to three seaside towns over a five-month period.*
>
> *Summarise the information by selecting and reporting the main features, and make comparisons where relevant.*

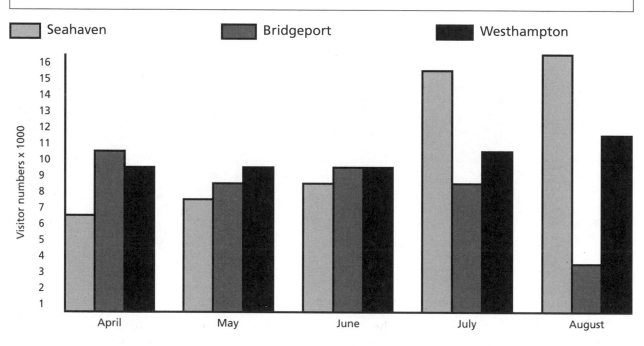

Seahaven   Bridgeport   Westhampton

Visitor numbers x 1000

April   May   June   July   August

<u>Sample answer</u>

The graph shows how many people visited three seaside towns between April and August.

The number of visitors to Seahaven (1) *increased* (2) .... between April and June, then (3) .... (4) .... in July, and continued to (5) .... in August. For the first four months, visitor numbers to Bridgeport (6) .... , but then (7) .... (8) .... in the final month. Westhampton visitor numbers (9) .... from April to June, then (10) .... (11) .... in July and finally (12) .... 11,000 in August.

Overall, there was an (13) .... in the number of visitors to Seahaven and Westhampton, but a (14) .... in the number of people visiting Bridgeport.

1 Complete these sentences with the correct form of one of the verbs in the box. Both sentences in each sentence pair should use the same verb. In some cases, the meaning of the verb may change slightly.

adjust	~~alter~~	deteriorate	exchange	fade	reduce	renovate
swell	switch	vary				

1. Moving to the countryside radically *altered* our lifestyle.

   Some people choose to *alter* their appearance with surgery.

2. By .... to a different provider, it can be possible to pay much less for your mobile phone bills.

   I chose drama as an extra-curricular activity, but .... to photography a few weeks later.

3. It can take time to .... to living in a different country.

   Prices seem low, but when you .... them to allow for tax, they are considerably higher.

4. The noise built up rapidly, and then just as quickly it .... into the distance.

   As the applause ...., the speaker started talking.

5. The amount of tax you pay on a car .... according to the amount of carbon dioxide it emits.

   People's reactions to the medicine .... a lot, with some people complaining it has no effect at all.

6. Everyone should try to .... the amount of fat in their diet.

   Many companies were forced to .... their workforce during the recession.

7. Economic crises often .... into social unrest.

   The weather .... rapidly when it started raining and the winds picked up.

8. Ankles and other joints often .... when people travel by air.

   The town is home to 3,000 people, but this figure .... to 12,000 in the same summer.

9. The tokens can be .... for food in the student canteen.

   Shops will normally .... damaged goods if you have a receipt.

10. Businesses in the city centre were offered funding so they could .... their premises.

    In some cases it can be more expensive to .... an old building than knock it down and build a new one.

Changes 2

2 Now do the same with these.

adapt cut decline disappear expand improve promote relax replace transform

1. Email has largely .... the traditional letter as a means of written business communication.

   The plan is to .... all the old desktop computers in the library with netbooks.

2. Some companies are slow to .... to a changing market.

   Courses can be .... to suit the needs of individual students.

3. The symptoms of illnesses like measles aren't usually serious, and .... within a few days.

   As the sun .... behind the clouds, the temperature quickly dropped.

4. A college course can help you to find a job or get .... at work.

   The 'Peter Principle' is a theory which says that in a big company, everyone eventually gets .... to a job that is beyond their ability.

5. Some people think that the government should .... the rules regarding building on protected land.

   For the final part of the exercise, you need to repeatedly tighten, then .... your stomach muscles.

6. The government's aim in the next five years is to .... educational standards.

   The best way of .... your English is to practise using it as much as possible.

7. Water freezes in the pipes, forcing them to .... and burst.

   Britain's universities .... at an unprecedented rate at the end of the twentieth century.

8. Supermarkets .... prices on many basic items to attract more customers.

   I believe that governments should increase spending on the arts instead of .... it.

9. Email and social networking websites have .... the way people communicate.

   When it was closed down, the old fire station was .... into an art gallery.

10. House prices are so high that the number of people buying their own home has .... in the last five years.

    Because so many people are out of work, living standards are .... rapidly.

1 Complete the second sentence in each pair so that it has the same or a similar meaning to the first sentence. Use the words or phrases in bold, and any other words that are necessary.

1. You can borrow my dictionary if you return it before you go home.

    providing that

    You can borrow my dictionary _providing that you return_ it before you go home.

2. I should get my assignment finished this weekend if I have enough time.

    provided that

    I should get my assignment finished this weekend .... enough time.

3. You can't go to university if you don't get good exam grades at school.

    unless

    You can't go to university .... good exam grades at school.

4. Students can use the common room in the evening if they tidy up any mess they make.

    on condition that

    Students can use the common room in the evening .... up any mess they make.

5. Pollution will get worse if we continue to live in a throwaway society.

    as long as

    Pollution will get worse .... to live in a throwaway society.

6. Children will always prefer fast food to fresh fruit and vegetables, even if you tell them how unhealthy it is.

    no matter how

    Children will always prefer fast food to fresh fruit and vegetables, ... tell them it is unhealthy.

7. Computer programming is complicated, even if you read a lot of books about it.

    however many

    Computer programming is complicated, ... read about it.

8. Crime is a problem, even if you live in a small town or in the countryside.

    wherever

    Crime is a problem, ... live.

2 Complete these sentences using an appropriate word or phrase from above and your own ideas.

1. British universities will accept students from abroad ....

    ....

2. Working for a large company can be a fulfilling experience ....

    ....

3. The environmental situation will continue to worsen ....

    ....

4. Travelling helps you understand more about the world around you ....

    ....

Confusing words & false friends 1

Confusing words are two or more words which:

(a) have a similar meaning to each other but which are used in a different way

or

(b) are related to the same topic, but have a different meaning

or

(c) look similar, but have a different meaning.

False friends are words in English which have a similar-looking word in another language, but which have a different meaning.

Complete the following sentence pairs with the appropriate word.

1. **aboard / abroad**

   More and more people go *abroad* for their holiday.

   In 2002, she became the first woman to travel *aboard* the space shuttle *Discovery*.

2. **action / activity**

   We decided to take immediate .... when we realised there was a problem.

   The environmental changes in the area are the result of human ....

3. **advice / advise**

   Can you .... me on the best course of action to take?

   He offered me some excellent ....

4. **affect / effect**

   Diverting the course of the river will have a major .... on the local ecosystem.

   Frequent traffic jams in the suburbs seriously .... journey times into the city.

5. **appreciable / appreciative**

   Widening the road made an .... difference to the flow of traffic.

   The applause at the end of the concert was warm and ....

6. **avoid / prevent**

   Rapid international action managed to .... an environmental disaster from taking place.

   There are areas in the city that are wise to .... after dark.

7. **beside / besides**

   The company's main office is .... the railway station.

   .... their regular daytime job, many people do extra work in the evening.

8. **briefly /shortly**

   .... before the earthquake began, many animals were seen to be behaving in an unusual manner.

   She spoke .... but passionately about the need to help those in developing countries.

9. **canal / channel**

   A .... system joined the two main rivers, which made transporting goods much quicker.

   When television first became popular in the early 1950s, there was only one ....

10. **conscientious / conscious**

   Most people are .... of the need to protect the environment.

   .... workers should be rewarded for their hard work.

11. **considerable / considerate**

   In my opinion, some people are not very .... of those around them.

   A .... amount of money was spent on developing the product.

12. **continual / continuous**

   The computer system has given us .... problems ever since we installed it. Some days it works, other days it doesn't.

   The .... noise from the new motorway has forced many people to move.

13. **control / inspect**

   New teachers often find it difficult to............... their classes.

   Environmental health inspectors regularly .... commercial kitchens for cleanliness, especially those in restaurants.

14. **criticism / objection**

   I have no .... to people using their mobile phones on buses or trains.

   Plans for the new stadium have attracted fierce .... from local people.

15. **damage / harm / injury**

   He suffered a serious .... which needed immediate hospital treatment.

   The low levels of dangerous chemicals in the river were enough to cause .... to aquatic life.

   A lot of .... was caused to buildings along the coast during the storm.

16. **during / for / while**

   The college closes .... two weeks at the end of December.

   He died .... trying to cross the desert alone.

   Many creatures stay underground .... daylight hours.

17. **however / moreover**

   The plan was good in theory. ...., in practice it was extremely difficult to implement.

   The plan was excellent. ...., it was clear from the beginning that it was going to attract a lot of interest.

18. **injured / wounded**

   I believe that we should do more to help and support soldiers who have been .... in combat.

   Several workers were .... when the drilling platform collapsed.

Confusing words & false friends 2

Complete the following sentence pairs with the appropriate word or phrase.

1. **job / work**

   Everybody has the right to a decent .... with good pay.

   During the economic recession, a lot of people found themselves out of ....

2. **lay / lie**

   If you're suffering from dehydration, you should drink plenty of water and sit or .... down for a while.

   Before you begin the experiment, you should .... a large plastic sheet on the ground.

3. **look at / watch**

   We need to .... the situation carefully over the next few weeks and see how things develop.

   We need to .... the problem carefully and decide if there is anything we can do about it.

4. **loose / lose**

   Some people are very competitive and hate to ....a game or competition.

   The surface is mainly composed of .... soil and small stones.

5. **make / cause**

   The noise from traffic outside the school can .... it hard to hear what the teacher is saying.

   Hurricanes .... widespread damage in urban areas.

6. **nature / countryside**

   Thousands of .... lovers head for the national parks every weekend.

   I'd rather live in the .... than in a city.

7. **per cent / percentage**

   It is a myth that only ten .... of Americans hold a passport.

   Only a small .... of land is privately owned.

8. **permission / permit**

   I'm afraid we can't .... photography in the museum.

   We received .... to attend the meeting, as long as we didn't interrupt.

9. **personal / personnel**

   My own .... view is that professional football players are paid far too much.

   The company was in trouble until there was a change of .... on the management team.

10. **possibility / chance**

    We might go to Spain for our field trip. Another .... is that we'll go to Italy instead.

    If we act now, we have a good .... of finding a cure for the disease.

Confusing words & false friends 2

11. **practice / practise**

   It's important to .... your English whenever possible.

   I think I need more .... before I take the exam.

12. **priceless / worthless**

   .... paintings by artists like Van Gogh and Rembrandt should not be in the hands of private collectors.

   As inflation spiralled out of control, paper money suddenly became almost ....

13. **principal / principle**

   Many people refuse to eat meat on ....

   She was appointed University .... in 2009.

   The country's .... food products are coffee and sugar.

   I believe in the .... that healthcare should be free for everyone.

14. **problem / trouble**

   At night, the streets are full of people fighting and generally causing ....

   I was wondering if you could help me with a little .... I'm having.

15. **process / procession**

   The highlight of the carnival is a huge .... along the town's main street.

   In some cases, applying for a visa can be a long and frustrating ....

16. **raise / rise**

   As prices ...., demand usually drops.

   In response to the oil crisis, most airlines had to .... their fares.

17. **remember / remind**

   I can .... my first day at school really well.

   Language teachers often .... their students that the best way to remember new words is to use them as much as possible.

18. **respectable / respectful**

   We all listened in .... silence as she outlined her plans for the museum's future.

   Everybody wants to bring their children up in a .... neighbourhood.

19. **tolerable / tolerant**

   People need to be more .... of their neighbours, and not complain every time they make too much noise.

   The local authorities say that the noise from passing trains is ...., but many living near the railway lines disagree.

20. **treat / cure**

   Many hospitals are so understaffed that they are refusing to .... patients with minor injuries.

   The new drug was unable to .... the disease, and hundreds died as a result.

Context & meaning 1

When we see a new word (in a reading passage, for example), we can often work out what it means, or get an *idea* of what it means, by looking at the context in which it appears (for example, what is the *passage* about, what is the *sentence* about and what information comes before and after the word?).

Identifying the meaning of a word from its context is an especially useful skill in the IELTS Reading Test.

1 Look at these words, and answer the questions which follow.

> nocturnal   cites   coherently   feat

1. Without seeing them in a sentence, do you know (or can you guess) what the words in the box mean?

nocturnal:	Yes / No	cites:	Yes / No
coherently:	Yes / No	feat:	Yes / No

2. Now look at the words in the passage. Can you guess what they mean now? In your own words, explain what they might mean.

> The remarkable success of Simon Weber's book on owls, bats, foxes and other **nocturnal** creatures, *A Call in the Dark*, is probably not surprising in view of the popularity of his recent television series, 'Night Prowlers'. It is a very thorough book by an author who is an expert in his field and who has clearly done a lot of research. In addition to describing his own findings, he **cites** the research carried out by others, including Wright and Lawson in the 1990s, and discusses where they might have gone wrong with some of their assumptions. He writes **coherently** on the subject, beginning by looking at basic facts before discussing progressively complex theories, without once confusing his readers. This is a remarkable **feat**, considering the complexity of the subject and the science that is often involved.

nocturnal: ....

cites: ....

coherently: ....

feat: ....

2 Look at the words in bold in sentences 1 – 15, and try to decide what they mean.

1. The journey across the hills was long and **arduous**, much of it having to be done on foot in temperatures of over 40°C.

2. Foxes are a common sight in our towns and cities, where they **forage** in dustbins, in gardens and on waste ground.

3. The cuckoo is a rare and **elusive** bird which is often heard but rarely seen.

4. The research they carried out was **exhaustive**, so by the time the project was complete, they knew everything they had to know about their subject.

5. The hotel we stayed in was a **mediocre** place, with small rooms, rather dull food and an uninspiring view of a car park.

6. Research suggests that children are more **resilient** than adults when it comes to getting over an illness.

7. The room was extremely untidy, with **stacks** of books and piles of paper all over the floor, and unwashed coffee cups on the tables.

8. He was an extremely **prolific** author, writing three or four novels a year as well as many short stories.

9. Water is essential for human life, so it is **imperative** we make sure that in the future there is enough for everyone.

10. Attempts to **implement** change met with strong resistance at first, but gradually people realised that this change was needed.

11. Many men say that they are willing to share the **burden** of domestic duties like washing and cooking, but I doubt that they mean it.

12. The building is designed to **sway** slightly in strong winds, but it's still a rather frightening sensation when you are on the upper floors.

13. Many people would like to own a house in the city centre, but **prohibitive** property prices mean that very few of them would ever be able to buy such a place.

14. The city centre has some beautiful old buildings, but there are some extremely ugly industrial estates on the **fringe**.

15. Employees are encouraged to use their **initiative** when they are faced with a problem and there is nobody more senior there to help them.

3 Now match the words in bold in sentences 1 – 15 above with their definitions (a) – (o) below.

(a)   A serious or difficult responsibility that you have to deal with. *burden*

(b)   Producing a lot of things, ideas, etc. ....

(c)   The ability to decide what to do in an independent way. ....

(d)   Able to quickly become healthy, happy or strong again. ....

(e)   Move or swing slightly from side to side. ....

(f)   Difficult or impossible to catch or find. ....

(g)   Make something such as in idea, plan, system, etc., start to work. ....

(h)   Extremely difficult and involving a lot of effort. ....

(i)   The outer edge of something. ....

(j)   So expensive that nobody can afford it. ....

(k)   Thorough and complete. ....

(l)   To search in a wide area for something, especially food. ....

(m)   Piles of things placed one on top of another. ....

(n)   Extremely important and urgent. ....

(o)   Average or below average. ....

Context & meaning 2

1 Read these sentences carefully, and decide if the definitions in *italics* of the words in bold are <u>correct</u> or <u>incorrect</u>. If they are incorrect, try to give a correct definition. The first one has been done as an example.

1. I'm worried that a lack of suitable qualifications will **hinder** my search for a job.

    Help someone or something, or make something easier.   Correct / <u>Incorrect</u>

    Hinder means to stop someone or something from making progress or developing.

2. Research was going well, but there was a risk that cuts in funding would **jeopardise** the entire project.

    Risk damaging or destroying something important.   Correct / Incorrect

3. When you **address** a meeting, it is important to speak clearly, confidently and at a good pace.

    Write a letter to someone.   Correct / Incorrect

4. The villas were basically **flimsy** wooden huts that shook every time there was a bit of wind.

    Strong and well built or made.   Correct / Incorrect

5. Although several species of turtle can be found in relatively cool seas, warm water provides the **optimal** conditions for breeding.

    The best or most suitable within a range of possibilities.   Correct / Incorrect

6. It can be very difficult for immigrants to **integrate** into local society, especially if there are marked cultural differences.

    Meet people or make useful contacts.   Correct / Incorrect

7. From the **outset** of the expedition they knew they were going to have problems, so it was no surprise when only two days later things started to go very wrong.

    The end of something.   Correct / Incorrect

8. He was a talented young film director whose unique and **innovative** style inspired generations of film students.

    Difficult to understand.   Correct / Incorrect

9. The building is 200 metres tall and **tapers** gently to a point, giving it the appearance of a thin, glass pyramid.

    Gradually becomes wider towards one end.   Correct / Incorrect

10. There are one or two similarities between my country and the UK, but on the whole they are so **disparate** that it is difficult to find any common ground.

    Having many differences.   Correct / Incorrect

11. Most modern furniture is functional but not especially **aesthetic**, especially when compared with some of the beautiful and elegant designs of the past.

    Cheap but comfortable.   Correct / Incorrect

12. Shops know that they can attract more customers if they have a large **array** of colourful products on display by or near the main entrance.

    A large group of people or things.   Correct / Incorrect

2 Now do the same with these.

1. The track has a **coarse** surface, providing better grip for bicycle tyres and making them less likely to skid on tight corners.

    Soft and smooth.   Correct / Incorrect

2. The idea of a tunnel under the sea was first **propagated** by engineers in the nineteenth century, but it was almost 200 years before it became a reality.

    Designed and built.   Correct / Incorrect

3. Everyone was in favour of making the city centre traffic free, but public opinion **shifted** when locals realised that vehicles would need to be diverted through residential areas.

    Changed or moved.   Correct / Incorrect

4. People like the new system, but because of the costs involved we do not believe it is **viable**, and we need to look for other options.

    Popular with people.   Correct / Incorrect

5. Some of Shakespeare's plays are often **attributed** to other writers, although more recent research suggests that they were all his own work.

    Given to someone else as a gift, donation, etc.   Correct / Incorrect

6. Although the inventor had a **patent** for his new product, other companies rapidly began copying and selling it, and he was forced to take legal action against them.

    An award or prize.   Correct / Incorrect

7. Spiders usually trap their **prey** in webs, but others actively hunt for it.

    An animal that is caught and eaten by another animal.   Correct / Incorrect

8. Some illnesses are serious enough to require medical treatment, but for minor health problems, a visit to the doctor is usually not **warranted**.

    To be unable to do something.   Correct / Incorrect

9. We need to come up with a **radical** solution to the problem of crime in our towns and cities, since everything else seems to have failed.

    New and very different from the usual way.   Correct / Incorrect

10. During the meeting, we made progress on **peripheral** issues, but unfortunately we failed to deal with the issues that had been causing us the most problems.

    The main or most important part of something.   Correct / Incorrect

11. I hate flying, and nothing could **induce** me to get on an aeroplane.

    Stop or prevent something.   Correct / Incorrect

12. There were several small problems with the original device, and it needed to be **refined** slightly before it could go on sale.

    Turned off and then on again.   Correct / Incorrect

Context & meaning 3

Sometimes, in addition to its context, we can work out what a word means from 'clues' in the word itself. These clues are usually in the form of one or two words (or parts of words) that we already know, often with the addition of prefixes and / or suffixes.

For example:

Healthcare = health + care
The town lacks basic <u>healthcare</u> facilities, so people have to travel many miles to see a doctor.

Deforestation = de + forest + ation.
<u>Deforestation</u> has resulted in the destruction of thousands of acres of tropical forest.

Facial = face + ial (the e is removed)
The company started off producing a range of <u>facial</u> cleansers and moisturisers which had not been tested on animals.

1 Can you work out what the words in bold in these sentences mean? Check your answers at the back of the book.

1. The country is very poor, and one in seven children dies in **infancy**.

2. All the employees are asked to produce a written evaluation of their performance and hand it to the **personnel** manager.

3. The new drug does not cure the illness, but can **prolong** the patient's life by up to five years.

4. The farm was on top of a **windswept** hill, miles from the nearest town.

5. Oil prices increased **threefold** over a five-year period.

6. The historical document has been examined by several distinguished **scholars**, but none of them can tell if it is genuine or fake.

7. When you deliver the package, make sure that the **recipient** signs for it.

8. The **centrepiece** of the new museum is a Henry Moore sculpture that was bought from a private collector.

9. The city offers a **multitude** of interesting and exciting activities for people of all ages.

10. Government statistics on the **numeracy** skills of ten-year-olds suggests that more emphasis needs to be placed on the teaching of mathematics in school.

11. The average **lifespan** of an elephant is 60 – 70 years.

12. Several interesting objects were found during the archaeological dig, but none of them were of any great **monetary** value.

13. From the top of the tower, we looked out over a city of incredible **grandeur**.

14. From a traveller's **standpoint**, the competition between airlines to win customers is a good thing.

2 Now do the same with these.

1. The city was over 60 miles from the **epicentre** of the earthquake, but still suffered substantial damage.

2. In some cases, hospital **outpatients** have to wait over three hours to see a doctor.

3. To many, the evidence he provided did not **validate** his claim that the Earth moved around the Sun.

4. Many medical professionals are concerned about the **widespread** use of antibiotics to treat minor medical conditions.

5. Modern **seafarers** rely on modern technology to help them navigate the oceans.

6. After the accident, he temporarily lost **spatial** awareness, and could only pick up objects when he closed one eye.

7. A **monorail** connects the airport with the city, taking visitors into the heart of the city in less than 20 minutes.

8. A new device which stimulates the **auditory** areas of the brain offers hope to those who have serious hearing problems.

9. I don't consider myself to be particularly **industrious**, but when I'm given a job, I make sure it gets done.

10. When, on his 104th birthday, he was asked about the secret to his **longevity**, he replied that he only ever ate raw vegetables and had never smoked.

11. The new airliner is more environmentally-friendly than other aircraft, its only **drawback** being its limited flying range.

12. The Museum of Contemporary Art **showcases** all that is best about modern art.

13. The Alaskan **wilderness** is not a place you want to be when winter comes.

14. In this remote, poverty-stricken area, only a few children go to school, and consequently about a quarter of the country's population is **illiterate**.

Contrast & comparison

Complete these sentences with the most appropriate word or phrase from A, B or C.

1. The two machines _differ_ considerably. One has an electric motor, the other runs on oil.
   A. differ   **B. differentiate**   **C. differential**

2. The .... in weather between the north and the south of the country is very noticeable.
   A. comparison   **B. contrast**   **C. compare**

3. Many people cannot .... between lemon juice and lime juice.
   A. differ   **B. differentiate**   **C. contrast**

4. Children must be taught to .... between right and wrong.
   A. differ   **B. contrast**   **C. distinguish**

5. There is a .... between being interested in politics and joining a political party.
   A. distinguish   **B. distinctive**   **C. distinction**

6. Can you tell the .... between a good boss and a bad one?
   A. difference   **B. differentiate**   **C. contrast**

7. The management must not .... between male and female applicants.
   A. differ   **B. contrast**   **C. discriminate**

8. Asia covers a huge area. .... , Europe is very small.
   A. By way of contrast   **B. By ways of comparing**   **C. By similar means**

9. The new model of car is very .... to the old one.
   A. same   **B. similar**   **C. common**

10. Her political opinions are .... to mine.
    A. same   **B. exactly**   **C. identical**

11. Some political parties have such similar manifestoes that they are difficult to
    ....
    A. tell apart   **B. say apart**   **C. speak apart**

12. My friends and I enjoy doing many of the same things. In that respect, we have a lot
    ....
    A. in similar   **B. in particular**   **C. in common**

13. There seems to be a large .... between the number of people employed in service industries, and those employed in the primary sector.
    A. discriminate   **B. discretion**   **C. discrepancy**

14. The nation's economy is largely based on its industry, ... a few hundred years ago it was an agrarian country.
    A. while   **B. whereas**   **C. whereby**

15. British and Australian people share the same language, but in other respects they are as different as ....
    A. cats and dogs   **B. chalk and cheese**   **C. salt and pepper**

Emphasis & misunderstanding

1 (Emphasis) Match the sentences on the left with an appropriate sentence on the right.

1. The committee's *emphasis* on the word 'recycling' was noticeable.

2. Our guide *accentuated* the importance of remaining calm if there was trouble.

3. Our teacher explained that it was *crucially important* to pace ourselves while revising for the exam.

4. At the conference, the *accent* was on unemployment.

5. *Prominent* scientists have stated that genetically modified food is probably perfectly safe.

6. It is *of crucial importance* that we make more use of technology if we are to make progress.

A. Some, however, are *emphatic* that more research needs to be carried out.

B. She *emphasised* the fact that panicking would only make matters worse.

C. The main speaker *gave prominence* in his speech to the need for better job opportunities.

D. We consider progress in this field to be *extremely important.*

E. He *put great stress* on the maxim that 'All work and no play makes Jack a dull boy'.

F. They *stressed* again and again the importance of reusing things as much as possible.

2 (Emphasis) Complete these sentences with a word or phrase in bold from exercise 1. You may need to change the form of the word or phrase. In some cases, more than one answer is possible.

1. Painting the building white did not make it look any better. In fact, it only .... its ugliness.

2. The rugged hills are a .... feature of the landscape

3. At the meeting of the Students' Council, the .... was on better standards of accommodation.

4. The Minister of Transport .... on the need for an integrated transport policy.

5. It is .... that we try to improve relations between our countries.

6. She banged the table for .... as she spoke.

3 (Misunderstanding) Complete these sentences with an appropriate word or expression from the box. In some cases, more than one answer is possible.

> assumed   confused   confusion   impression   misapprehension
>
> mistaken   mix-up   obscure

1. I was completely .... by his explanation, and had to ask someone else what he meant.

2. There were scenes of .... at the airport when the snowstorm stopped all the flights.

3. We nearly didn't catch our flight because of a .... over the tickets.

4. There are several .... points in your essay. It's not very clear.

5. He was under the .... that socialism and communism were the same thing.

6. We all ...., wrongly as it turned out, that we would be interviewed individually.

7. Many people are .... in the belief that organic food is better for you than conventionally-grown food.

8. She gave us the .... that we had done something to upset her, although we had done nothing of the sort.

Focusing attention

1 Rearrange the letters in bold to form words which are used to focus attention on something. They all end with the letters -ly. Write the words in the grid underneath. If you do it correctly, you will find another word used to focus attention in the bold vertical box.

1. They reduced pollution *psimly* by banning cars from the city centre during the rush hour.
2. I come from a *galerly* rural community where life moves at a slower pace.
3. We're *iimprarly* examining the financial aspects of the case.
4. People *inamly* go on holiday in the summer.
5. The college library is *veceslxuily* for the use of students and staff.
6. It's a *ilaptarrculy* difficult problem which we hope to resolve as soon as possible.
7. The advertisement is *elcifipcsaly* aimed at people over 50.
8. Some western countries, *otbanly* Canada and the United States, have a very high standard of living.
9. The tourists who visit my town are *stomly* Australian.
10. Our trip to Poland was *rpeuly* an educational visit.
11. My home town is famous *hfiecly* for its large number of schools and colleges.

| 1. | S | I | | M | | P | L | | Y | | | | | | |

The word in the in the bold vertical box fits into this sentence:

The company trades .... in the Far East.

2 Divide the words above into two groups, one group being the words which mean _only_ or _solely_, and one group being the words which mean _in most cases_, _normally_ or _the main reason for something_.

<u>Only</u> or <u>solely</u>	<u>In most cases</u>, <u>normally</u> or the <u>main reason for something</u>
simply	chiefly

1 Match the sentences in the first list below with an appropriate sentence in the second list on the next page. The _underlined words and phrases_ in the first list should have a similar meaning to the words and phrases in bold in the second list. Write the sentence letter (A, B, C, etc.) from the second list after the relevant sentence in the first list.

FIRST LIST

1. **_Small items of information_** are very important in a curriculum vitae. _D_.

2. I need to have **_precise information_** about your new proposals. ....

3. The plan was unable to go ahead because of a **_small important detail which is important in order to make something happen_**. ....

4. He demanded to know the **_small, precise and sometimes unimportant details_**. ....

5. When you read a piece of text in the exam, you should read it quickly first to get the **_general idea_**. ....

6. Before you write an essay, you should plan it first and give a broad **_description without giving much detail_**. ....

7. **_Odd features or details which make something different_** make the world a more interesting place. ....

8. Saying that all young people spend too much time on the Internet is a bit of a **_general statement_**. ....

9. Many cars have very similar **_typical features_**. ....

10. The huge rise in computer sales is a good **_example_** of the direction in which technology is heading. ....

11. **_Normally_**, most students sitting the exam manage to pass with a good grade. ....

12. The new library **_shows a good example of_** British architecture at its best. ....

13. Before you travel somewhere, it is important to **_make a detailed list of_** things that you need to take. ....

14. French fries with mayonnaise is a dish which is **_an odd feature or detail of_** Belgian cuisine. ....

15. The article **_shows as an example_** his views on the way the company should develop. ....

Generalisations & specifics

SECOND LIST

A. Please let me have **the specifics** as soon as possible.

B. It's very frustrating when a minor **technicality** puts a stop to your plans.

C. In the same way, kimchii is a concoction of cabbage, chilli and garlic which is **peculiar to** Korea.

D. You should include full **details** of your past experience.

E. Once you have an **outline,** you will discover that your work is easier to organise.

F. We must be careful not to make this kind of **generalisation.**

G. **Itemise** everything in order of importance, beginning with your passport and visa.

H. As far as he was concerned, the **minutiae** could not be overlooked.

I. Most manufacturers are aware that these **characteristics** are what help sell their product.

J. It also provides us with an accurate **illustration** of the advances we have made in the last 20 years.

K. It **illustrates** his preference for increased automation.

L. Once you have the **gist,** it should be easier to understand it.

M. It **exemplifies** the style that is becoming increasingly popular with town planners.

N. In **general,** the average result is a B or C.

O. For example, it is one of the **peculiarities** of the British system that judges and lawyers wear wigs in court.

2 Put the words and phrases above into the table below, based on whether they are talking about *specific* things or *general* things. Then try to use the words in sentences of your own.

Specific things:	*the specifics*
General things:	

1 Put these words into the table based on the things they usually refer to.

> batch   bunch   bundle   cast   company   crew   ~~crowd~~   flock
> gang   group   herd   huddle   pile   litter   pack   platoon   set
> shoal   stack   staff   swarm   team   throng

People in general	A group of people working together	Animals	Objects
crowd			

2 Complete these sentences using one of the words from Exercise 1. You may need to make your answer plural, and in some cases more than one answer is possible.

1. A .... of just 25 dairy cows can produce over a thousand litres of milk a day.

2. Just because a film has a .... of well-known actors, it does not necessarily mean it will be successful.

3. During the rainy season, huge .... of mosquitoes make life very uncomfortable for the local residents.

4. Shelf space in the library is so limited that there are .... of books all over the floor.

5. The coral reef is home to .... of colourful fish.

6. Airline cabin .... do much more than just serve food to passengers.

7. A simple .... of tools can cost the equivalent of a month's wages for some.

8. The college employs a .... of about 200.

9. A .... of flowers is always an acceptable gift if you visit someone.

10. During National Day celebrations, an enormous ....of people descended on the city's main square.

11. In some areas of the city, ... of wild dogs roam the streets at night

12. A small .... of people sat under the tree, trying to keep warm and dry.

13. You know winter is arriving when huge .... of geese and other birds can be seen heading south.

14. The bread oven can produce a .... of 200 loaves every hour.

15. Hundreds of migrant workers arrive in the city every day, many carrying no more than a small .... of clothes and other personal possessions.

16. .... of youths can often be seen hanging around on street corners looking for trouble.

How something works

1 Complete the descriptions of how these objects work with the correct form of the words and phrases in the boxes. In some cases, more than one answer may be possible.

1. A thermostat

adjust	bend	connect	contain	contract	cool down
disconnect	expand	heat up	turn off		

A thermostat *contains* a strip or coil of steel and a strip or coil of copper, one on top of the other. As the strip / coil ...., the metals ...., but one does it faster than the other. The strip / coil ....and ....with a switch, which .... the power supply. When the strip / coil ...., the metals .... and the switch is .... The thermostat is .... using a dial or other control.

2. A disc player

convert	decrease	hear	increase	insert	replace	spin
strike	view					

A disc player (for example, in a computer) has several component parts. A disc is .... into the player and begins to .... At the same time, a thin beam of light called a laser .... the disc and .... digital signals into sounds or images, which can be .... through speakers or .... on a screen. Volume or brightness can be .... or .... by means of a button, knob or other control. Nowadays, discs are largely being .... by storage devices like memory sticks, which have no moving parts.

3. An aerosol

compress	expand	leave	mix	open	push	release

In an aerosol, liquid and gas are .... in a metal and / or hard plastic tube. This can be .... from the tube by .... a button, which .... a valve. When the liquid-gas combination .... the tube and .... with oxygen, it rapidly ....

4. An aircraft

accelerate	create	flow	form	made	move	pull	produce

Most aircraft are .... of aluminium, and require two forces to allow them to fly: thrust and lift. As the aircraft .... forward on the ground under the power of its engines, air .... over the wings. As it .... faster, ... more thrust, a vacuum is .... over the wings. This .... lift. The aircraft is .... into the air by the force of this lift.

5. A digital camera

adjust	consist	control	download	enter	hit	open	press
record	store						

A digital camera .... of two main parts: a body and a lens. When a button is .... on the body, a window in the lens called a *shutter* .... and light .... the camera. The amount of light going into the camera is .... by both the speed of this shutter, and a smaller window called an *aperture*. Both the shutter speed and the size of the aperture can be .... by the person using the camera. The light .... a sensor in the body of the camera, which .... the light as a digital image. The image is .... on a memory card in the camera, and this can later be .... on to a computer.

Joining / becoming part of something bigger

The sentences below all contain a word or phrase in *italics* which is related to the idea of two or more things joining together, sometimes with the result that they become part of something bigger. However, the words and phrases have all been put into the wrong sentence. Put them into their correct sentence. In some cases, more than one answer is possible.

1 Write the correct verb at the end of each sentence.

1. His salary is *merged* to the cost of living, and increases on an annual basis. *linked*

2. The International Book Association *blended* with Universal Press in 2010 to form the International Press. ....

3. To get a better finish, he *swallowed up* the two paints together. ....

4. The firm *integrated* with its main competitor in the battle to win more customers. ....

5. The suggestions from all the committees were *took over* into the main proposal. ....

6. The immigrants faced hostility when they were first *incorporated* into the community. ....

7. A lot of students had problems before they *amalgamated* into college life. ....

8. When the large international college *got together* the smaller school, a lot of people lost their jobs. ....

9. The students *linked* one evening and decided to protest about their situation. ....

10. A large international company *assimilated* our firm last month and started making immediate changes. ....

2 Write the correct noun at the end of each sentence.

1. The *alloy* between England and France came close to breaking down many times during the nineteenth century. ....

2. The *synthesis* between England and Scotland is over 300 years old. ....

3. Last year, the three regional organisations responsible for helping homeless people formed a national *blend* to help and support one another. ....

4. Brass is a well-known *alliance* of copper and zinc. ....

5. Water is a *coalition* of hydrogen and oxygen. ....

6. The plan is a *unification* of several earlier proposals. ....

7. The *merger* of Italy did not occur until the second half of the nineteenth century. ....

8. The company made its fortune by selling a popular *union* of coffee. ....

9. The proposed *federation* of the Liberal and Labour Parties in the election was cause for much ridicule. ....

10. As a result of the *compound* with the other company, Flax International became the largest in its field. ....

Likes & dislikes

Decide if the words and phrases in bold in these sentences have a *positive connotation* (for example, they tell us that somebody likes or wants something) or a *negative connotation* (for example, they tell us that someone dislikes something). <u>Underline</u> the correct answer.

1. The idea of travelling around the world really **appeals to** me. <u>*Positive*</u> / *Negative*

2. Research suggests that shoppers are **attracted to** brightly-lit, colourful displays. *Positive* / *Negative*

3. I like him, but unfortunately he **can't stand** me. *Positive* / *Negative*

4. I can never understand why people are so **captivated by** royal weddings. *Positive* / *Negative*

5. A lot of people **detest** seafood, and some are even allergic to it. *Positive* / *Negative*

6. Bigoted people **disgust** me with their small-minded attitudes. *Positive* / *Negative*

7. He's a very punctual person, and **dreads** being late for anything. *Positive* / *Negative*

8. My brother **fancies** spending some time working abroad. *Positive* / *Negative*

9. I'm **fascinated by** new technology, and spend a lot of money on the latest electronic gadgets. *Positive* / *Negative*

10. She's **fond of** classical music, and would like to be a classical pianist. *Positive* / *Negative*

11. A lot of people are **keen on** football, but it doesn't interest me. *Positive* / *Negative*

12. We were cold and wet, and **longed for** a hot drink. *Positive* / *Negative*

13. I don't like early morning starts, and absolutely **loathe** having to get out of bed early. *Positive* / *Negative*

14. I always **look forward to** my English lessons. *Positive* / *Negative*

15. I'm **passionate about** flying, but rarely get the chance to go anywhere by plane. *Positive* / *Negative*

16. She's a vegetarian, and the thought of eating meat **repels** her. *Positive* / *Negative*

17. Supermarkets know that customers who come in for essential items like milk and bread are often **tempted by** special offers on other products. *Positive* / *Negative*

18. We had been working very hard, and were **yearning for** a holiday. *Positive* / *Negative*

Location & direction

1 Look at the map and town guide, and complete the sentences with the words and phrases in the box.

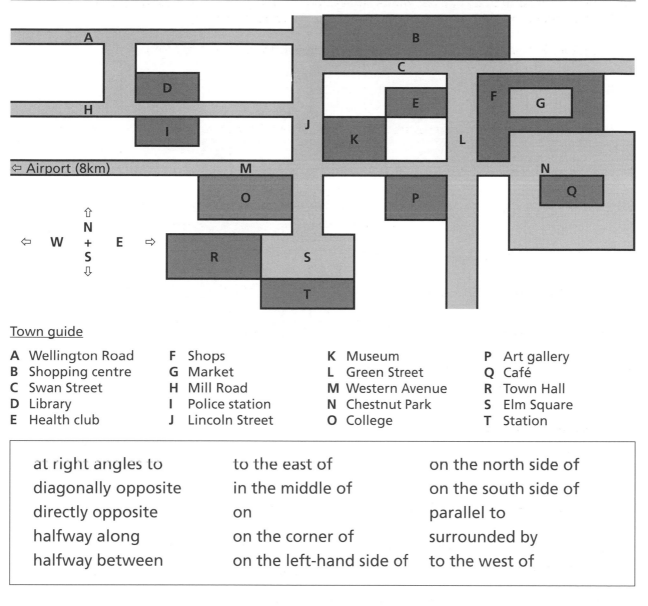

Town guide

A Wellington Road	**F** Shops	**K** Museum	**P** Art gallery
B Shopping centre	**G** Market	**L** Green Street	**Q** Café
C Swan Street	**H** Mill Road	**M** Western Avenue	**R** Town Hall
D Library	**I** Police station	**N** Chestnut Park	**S** Elm Square
E Health club	**J** Lincoln Street	**O** College	**T** Station

at right angles to	to the east of	on the north side of
diagonally opposite	in the middle of	on the south side of
directly opposite	on	parallel to
halfway along	on the corner of	surrounded by
halfway between	on the left-hand side of	to the west of

1. The library is .... the police station.

2. The airport is 8km .... the town.

3. The station is .... Elm Square.

4. Chestnut Park is .... the town.

5. The Town Hall is .... Elm Square.

6. The café is .... Chestnut Park.

7. The museum is .... Lincoln Street.

8. Wellington Road is .... Mill Road.

9. Swan Street is .... Lincoln Street.

10. The shopping centre is .... Swan Street.

11. Western Avenue is .... Elm Square and Mill Road.

12. The college is .... the museum.

13. The market is .... shops.

14. The health club is .... Green Street.

15. The art gallery is .... Western Avenue and Green Street.

Location & direction

2 Now look at this map and guide. Find where you are on it, then follow the directions to find out where you are going.

Town guide

A Hotel

B Internet café

C Post office

D Bank

E Supermarket

F Theatre

G Hairdresser

H Electrical store

I Bakery

J Travel agency

K Coffee shop

L Restaurant

M Cinema

N Language school

O Surgery

P Book shop

Q Mobile phone store

R Library

S Furniture store

T Department store

Directions: Go along the High Street, and turn left at the crossroads. Carry on and turn right at the end of the road. Go past the cinema and take the second road on your left. The place you want is the third building on your right.

You are going to ……………………..

Location & direction

3 Complete these directions using the words and phrases in the box. In each case, begin from the place labelled 'You are here'. You will need to use some words / phrases more than once.

crossroads	on your right
first	second
go along	take the first
go past	take the second
go to the end	the end
last	turn left
on your left	turn right

Directions to the supermarket

(1) .... of the High Street and (2) .... Go along this road and

(3) .... road (4) .... .The supermarket is the (5) ....

building (6) ....

Directions to the language school

(7) .... the High Street, and (8) .... at the (9) ....

(10) .... road (11) .... and the language school is the

(12) .... building (13) ....

Directions to the book shop

(14) .... the High Street and (15) .... at the (16) ....

Go to (17) .... of this road and (18) .... again, then

(19) .... road (20) .... (21) .... the library,

and the book shop is the (22) .... building (23) ....

4 Choose three other places on the map and write your own directions.

1. ....
   ....
   ....

2. ....
   ....
   ....

3. ....
   ....
   ....

Modified words

1 Modify (change) each word in bold in the sentences by adding a prefix from the box, so that the word is correct in the context of the sentence. Use each prefix once only.

auto	bi	circum	co	inter	micro	mono	over	post	pre
semi	sub	tele	trans	under	uni				

1. Thanks to Internet technology, companies can hold ....**conferences** with their agents and customers around the world without leaving the office.

2. The conference is a ....**annual** event, and usually takes place in March and September.

3. In her new ....**biography**, the travel writer and broadcaster Lucy Apps treats her readers to some fascinating tales about her life on the open road.

4. Email and social networking websites have ....**formed** the way people communicate.

5. Unfortunately, the project team exceeded its ....**determined** level of spending, and had to borrow more money.

6. Despite being knocked out of the World Cup in the ....**-final**, there was a great sense of elation, and the certainty that we would go all the way the next time.

7. Only a small percentage of students who do a university degree go on to do ....**graduate** studies.

8. People enjoy their jobs much more if they get on with their ....**-workers**.

9. If you knew about all the potentially dangerous ....**-organisms** that live on an average dishcloth, you would probably never use one again!

10. ....**sex** fragrances are believed to be a modern invention, but a century ago all perfumes were for men and women alike, and people just chose the one they liked the most.

11. If you feel that you have received ....**standard** service, you should complain to the manager or most senior employee immediately rather than wait until later.

12. In 1929, the Graf Zeppelin became the first airship to ....**navigate** the world.

13. Astronauts started living on the ....**national** Space Station in 2000.

14. I have two dictionaries: an English-French one, and a ....**lingual** English one.

15. I was an ....**achiever** at school, always getting low grades in tests and poor marks in my homework.

16. The city is so ....**populated** that it is almost impossible to find anywhere to live.

Modified words

2 Now do the same with these. Use the same prefixes from the box in Exercise 1.

1. ....**waves** work by passing electricity through food rather than by heating it.

2. The late twentieth century saw enormous advances in ....**communications**, with the development of the Internet being of particular importance.

3. In 1986, against everybody else's wishes, the ruling government made the ....**lateral** decision to close half the country's coal mines.

4. The suburbs consist of nothing but mile after mile of ....**-detached** houses and apartment blocks.

5. On long-distance flights, the aircraft is flown by ....**pilot** most of the time, with the real pilots only assuming occasional control.

6. I speak English and Spanish, but my Spanish is quite limited, so unfortunately I wouldn't say I'm ....**lingual**.

7. There are strict laws against advertising tobacco products, but with a bit of imagination, many of these can be easily ....**vented.**

8. A lot of the city was destroyed during the war, so during the immediate ....**-war** years, the government embarked on a massive reconstruction programme.

9. I think I passed my exams, but it would be ....**mature** to say that I've done well in all of them.

10. A third of the children were found to be ....**weight** as a result of a high-fat, high-sugar diet.

11. It is believed that many people who dislike water have a ....**conscious** fear of drowning.

12. Most of the schools in my country are ....**educational**, although there are a few boy-only and girl-only institutions.

13. We ran out of money because we had **estimated** how much the trip would cost.

14. The aviator Charles Lindbergh made the first solo ....**atlantic** flight in 1927.

15. Part of our course was to study the ....**relationship** between stress and illness, and especially to what extent one resulted in the other.

16. He knew a lot about his subject, but he spoke in such a dull ....**tone** that his students would often fall asleep.

Objects & actions

1 The verbs in the box describe the actions of the things in 1 – 18. Match each verb with the thing it describes.

congeal	crack	erode	evaporate	expand	explode	fade	
~~freeze~~	leak	rise	rotate	slide	smoulder	spill	spin	stretch
vibrate	wobble						

1. Water changing from a liquid to a solid state because of the cold. *freeze*

2. The drum in a washing machine moving very quickly in its final stage of a wash. ....

3. The disc tray opening and closing on a computer. ....

4. Water slowly turning into vapour. ....

5. Cooking fat or oil becoming solid on an unwashed plate. ....

6. The planet Earth moving around on its axis. ....

7. A loose wheel on a car. ....

8. Gas coming out of a faulty valve. ....

9. A pane of glass in a window frame when a large vehicle passes nearby. ....

10. A T-shirt which has been washed so often it is losing its colour. ....

11. The sun coming up in the morning. ....

12. Cliffs being slowly destroyed by the sea. ....

13. Slightly damp wood on a fire giving off smoke but no flames. ....

14. Cold metal as it gets hotter. ....

15. A piece of elastic being pulled so that it becomes longer. ....

16. A window being hit by a stone so that a long, thin break forms in the glass. ....

17. Coffee falling out of a cup by mistake. ....

18. A bomb suddenly blowing up. ....

2 Now do the same with these.

bounce	burn	condense	contract	crumble	erupt	float	flow
grow	meander	melt	revolve	ring	set	sink	spread	subside
trickle							

1. The Earth moving around the Sun. ....

2. A house slowly sinking into soft ground. ....

3. Traffic moving smoothly along a motorway. ....

4. Glass changing from a solid to a liquid in very high heat. ....

5. A rubber ball hitting the ground and going back into the air. ....

6. The population of a town becoming bigger. ....

7. The sun going down in the evening. ....

8. Gas or steam changing into a liquid. ....

9. A wide river going through the countryside in big curves. ....

10. Documents being laid out on a table. ....

11. Water coming very slowly out of a tap. ....

12. A slice of bread in a toaster turning black and beginning to give off smoke. ....

13. A lump of dry earth being rubbed between somebody's fingers. ....

14. Hot metal as it gets cooler. ....

15. An old-fashioned alarm clock suddenly going off. ....

16. A boat going to the bottom of a river. ....

17. Dead fish lying on the surface of a polluted lake. ....

18. A volcano throwing out lava and ash. ....

3 Some of the words in Exercise 1 and 2 can be used in more than one way, often with a different meaning. Complete these sentences with an appropriate word (the definition of the word you need in *italics* after each sentence will help you). You will need to change the form of some of the words.

1. The company *froze* its employees wages until the end of the year. (*to say officially that the rate or level of something must stay the same and not increase*)

2. Some people .... through life without really knowing what they want to do. (*to behave in a way that shows you do not have a clear plan for what you want to do*)

3. Food prices have been .... steadily all year. (*to increase in amount*)

4. As the light .... in the evening, people start coming out onto the street. (*to become less bright*)

5. He managed to .... a two-hour presentation into 30 minutes. (*to make something shorter or smaller*)

6. As the storms slowly died out, the floodwaters gradually .... (*to become lower*)

7. The discussion we had last night .... around the problem of finding affordable accommodation. (*to have something as the main or most important part of a subject*)

8. You can .... the machine to turn itself on or off at a particular time. (*to make a piece of equipment ready to operate*)

9. As soon the company's website went on-line, orders began to .... in. (*to arrive or leave in small amounts or numbers*)

10. The queue for tickets was so long it .... all the way down the street. (*to continue for a long distance*)

11. Once a week we get together and .... ideas off each other. (*to discuss ideas with other people in order to get their opinion and make a decision*)

12. They wanted to keep the story secret, but someone .... it to the press. (*to give private or secret information to journalists or to the public*)

Obligation & option

1 Look at sentences 1 – 10 and decide if the explanation which follows each one is true or false. <u>Underline</u> the correct answer. Use the words and phrases in bold to help you decide.

1. During the exam, a pencil and eraser are **required**.
    The people organising the exam will provide you with a pencil and an eraser. **True / <u>False</u>**

2. Parents can be made **liable for** their children's debts.
    Parents may be legally responsible for the money their children owe. **True / False**

3. He was **obliged to** pay back the money that he had won.
    He had the choice whether or not to pay back the money that he had won. **True / False**

4. Students doing holiday jobs are **exempt from** paying income tax.
    Students doing holiday jobs pay a smaller amount of income tax than other people. **True / False**

5. The United Nations voted to impose **mandatory** sanctions on the country.
    The United Nations imposed legally-binding sanctions which had to be obeyed by everyone, without exception. **True / False**

6. Some companies **force** their employees to work long hours for low pay.
    A lot of companies ask their employees to work long hours. **True / False**

7. It was an emergency and she pressed the red button; there was **no alternative.**
    There was nothing else she could do; she had to set off the alarm by pressing the red button. **True / False**

8. Classes on Wednesday afternoons are **optional.**
    It is necessary to attend classes on Wednesday afternoons. **True / False**

9. It is **compulsory** to wear a crash helmet on a motorcycle.
    It is your choice whether or not to wear a crash helmet when you ride a motorcycle. **True / False**

10. The museum is asking visitors for a **voluntary** donation of £2.
    You don't need to pay £2 to visit the museum. **True / False**

2 Complete these sentences with an appropriate word or phrase from the exercise above. In some cases, more than one answer may be possible.

1. Visitors to the country are .... to declare any excess tobacco or alcohol imports to the customs officer.

2. I'm afraid I have .... but to resign from the committee.

3. If you are caught speeding, you will be .... the payment of the fine.

4. Attendance at all classes is .... , otherwise you may not get a certificate at the end of the course.

5. Many retired people do .... work in their local community.

6. In some countries, there is a .... death sentence for all drug traffickers.

7. For visitors to Britain from outside the European Union, a visa may be ....

8. I hate it when people try to .... me to do something I don't like.

9. Most new cars come with .... air-conditioning.

10. Children's clothes are .... from VAT.

34

Opinion, attitude & belief

1 The words in *italics* in the following sentences are all grammatically incorrect (for example, a noun has been used instead of an adjective, or a verb has been used instead of a noun, etc.). Decide what the correct form of the word should be in each sentence, and write your answers in the crossword on the next page.

1. I think that people need to show greater *tolerate* of each other.

2. Some major companies are *obsession* with secrecy.

3. I *reckoning* that global warming is having more of an effect than we think.

4. We strongly *suspicious* that the proposal to develop the computer facilities will be rejected.

5. Some people are extremely *bigotry*, especially regarding things like race or religion.

6. I very much *doubtful* that the situation will improve in the near future.

7. A lot of people are *fanatic* about sport in general and football in particular.

8. He was very hard-working and *dedication* to his research.

9. In my *opinionated*, people don't take enough exercise.

10. I consider myself to be a *pragmatist* person, and believe that results are more important than theories or ideas.

11. Team members need to be completely *commitment*, and prepared to work for long hours.

12. The government is *regardless* foreign debt, especially in developing countries, as a major barrier to global economic development.

13. People often indicate their *disapprove* of something through their body language rather than words.

14. I *maintenance* that many young people would rather work than continue with their studies.

15. As far as I am *concerning*, happiness is more important than money.

16. Unhappy people often have a *cynic* view of life.

17. I take strong *exceptional* to people coming late or cancelling appointments at short notice.

18. Many scientists are *convincingly* that human activity is threatening the future of many animal and plant species.

19. My parents are *tradition* people who believe that children should not have too much freedom.

20. He had very *conservatism* views and did not like change of any sort.

Opinion, attitude & belief

¹T ²O L E R A N C E

2 Complete these sentences with the words from Exercise 1. You will either need a word from the sentences *or* from the completed crossword. In some cases, more than one answer may be possible.

1. People are often .... of strangers, and refuse to trust anyone unless they know them very well.

2. She's very well organised, and always takes a .... approach to problem solving.

3. I'm absolutely .... about keeping fit, and go to the gym at least once a day.

4. I strongly .... of smoking, and refuse to let people smoke in my home.

5. My .... is that people who read a lot are more interesting than people who don't.

6. To succeed in life, you need ambition and ....

7. My father won't .... anyone who questions his decisions.

8. Small farm communities are predominantly .... in their outlook and behaviour.

9. Some people .... my ability to succeed, but I am determined to prove they are wrong.

10. A lot of people in my country .... that the current economic crisis will get worse before it gets better.

Opposites: adjectives

Replace the adjectives in bold in these sentences with a word from the box which has an opposite meaning in the context of the sentence.

approximate	~~clear~~	chronic	costly	crude	delicate	detrimental
dim	easy	even	flexible	graceful	innocent	marked
obligatory	reluctant	scarce	widespread			

1. The terms and conditions on the contract are **ambiguous**. _clear._

2. According to the people who knew him, he was a very **awkward** person to work with. ....

3. I had never seen a dancer who was so **clumsy**. ....

4. The changes he made were **beneficial** to the organisation as a whole. ....

5. We need **exact** figures before we decide if we can go ahead with the project. ....

6. Following a lengthy investigation, they decided that the company was **guilty**. ....

7. What do you get if you add up all the **odd** numbers between 1 and 100?. ....

8. Despite the weather, supplies of food after the harvest were **plentiful**. ....

9. There are very **rigid** laws regarding building on green belts around a city . ...

10. I've noticed a **slight** difference in his attitude over the last few weeks . ...

11. The villagers have designed a **sophisticated** device for turning dirty water into clean drinking water. ....

12. The spices used in the production of some international dishes have a very **strong** flavour. ....

13. The blackness of the night was broken by a **strong** orange light which was visible on the horizon. ....

14. Student attendance at extra-curricular activities is **voluntary**. ....

15. Most students say they are **willing** to attend classes on Saturday morning. ....

16. The tornado caused **localised** damage. ....

17. He made his fortune by importing **cheap** perfume and clothing material. ....

18. People with **mild** allergies to dust were advised to remain indoors and close their windows. ....

Opposites: verbs

Replace the verbs or verb phrases in bold in these sentences with a word from the box which has an opposite meaning in the context of the sentence. You will need to change the form of most of the verbs.

> abandon   accelerate   ~~accept~~   agree   defend   demolish   deny
> deteriorate   fall   forbid   ignore   loosen   lower   retain   retreat
> reward   simplify   withdraw

1. When our trip was cancelled, we **rejected** the travel company's offer of a partial refund. _accepted_

2. She **admitted** that she had left the door unlocked when she left the house. ....

3. Aerial footage shows how quickly the floodwaters are **advancing**. ....

4. The company **refused** to let members of the public enter the building. ....

5. Many shopkeepers **attacked** the decision to make the street traffic-free. ....

6. The factory was **built** in 2004. ....

7. He **complicated** matters by rewriting the original proposal. ....

8. When the money ran out, they had to decide whether or not to **continue with** their research. ....

9. Relations between the two countries have **improved** considerably in the last few years. ....

10. **Punishing** young children in order to get them to work hard is, in my opinion, wrong. ....

11. He **raised** the overall standards of the company within two months of his appointment. ....

12. Smoking is **allowed** in most restaurant and cafés. ....

13. Prices **rose** sharply in the first three months of the year. ....

14. Before you do anything else, make sure you **tighten** the knots in the rope. ....

15. I went to the bank and **deposited** over £5,000. ....

16. He **lost** his position as head of the department. ....

17. By pushing the red button, the vehicle **slows down** rapidly. ....

18. Everyone **acknowledged** all the hard work I had done. ....

Ownership, giving, lending & borrowing

1 Complete the sentences with an appropriate noun from the box. In some cases, more than one answer is possible.

> belongings   donation   estate   landlords   loan   mortgage
> owners   possessions   property   proprietors   rent   tenants

1. The law ensures that .... respect the privacy of the people who live in their houses and flats.

2. .... of restaurants across the country protested when the government announced it was going to impose a tax on some foods.

3. When private car .... sell their vehicle, they must produce a certificate to prove the car has been paid for in full.

4. The price of commercial .... in the city centre has doubled in the last three years.

5. Mornington Park, a 250-acre private .... in Wenfordshire, is open to members of the public at weekends.

6. Many families in the area lost their home and all of their .... when the river flooded.

7. Please put your .... in the lockers provided, and hand your key to the receptionist for safekeeping.

8. We took out a .... to help pay for our trip.

9. A lot of people lost their homes when interest rates rose so high they were unable to continue paying off their ....

10. Only a few people in the apartment block actually own their flat. Most of them are council ....

11. The law does very little to protect families who are evicted from their homes because they are unable to pay the monthly ....

12. I make a small monthly............... to a local charity for homeless people.

2 Most of the verbs in bold below are in the wrong sentence. If the verb is *correct*, put a tick (✓) at the end of the sentence. If the verb is *wrong*, write the correct verb at the end of the sentence.

1. Banks will usually refuse to **present** money to anyone unless they have a regular job. ....

2. The best way to see the country is to a **provide** car for a couple of weeks. ....

3. Companies who **allocate** heavily from banks to keep their business going are rarely able to pay it back. ....

4. If you want to **rent** a room in the city centre, you should be prepared to pay a lot of money. ....

5. After her speech, the principal will **lend** prizes to the students who have made the greatest contribution to the school. ....

6. I believe that everyone should **donate** money to charities. ....

7. Local councils will **borrow** accommodation to the most needy on a first-come, first-served basis. ....

8. Many charitable organisations **hire** free medical help and support to areas hit by disasters. ....

Phrasal verbs 1

Write a preposition(s) or particle(s) from the box after each verb in bold in these sentences to make phrasal verbs. The meaning of each phrasal verb is in italics at the end of each sentence.

back	behind	down	forward	in	into	of	off	on	out
over	to	up	with						

1. Some parents are criticised for the way they **bring** .... their children. *(raise)*

2. The committee members **fell** .... over plans for the new health centre. *(argued)*

3. They refused to **face** .... their responsibilities, with disastrous consequences. *(accept an unpleasant state of affairs, and try to deal with it)*

4. At the last minute we had to **call** .... our visit to the museum. *(not to go ahead with something)*

5. I can always **count** .... my best friend to be there when I need him. *(rely / depend)*

6. Many developing countries are failing to **catch** .... their more developed neighbours. *(get to the same level)*

7. As the wind **dies** ...., the heat and humidity gradually begin to rise. *(becomes less strong)*

8. An alarming number of students **drop** .... school early every year. *(leave)*

9. Major international companies can't **figure** .... the popularity of the anti-capitalist movement. *(find it hard to understand)*

10. If they examined the issues more closely, they would **find** .... the reasons for the changes. *(discover)*

11. As we **grow** .... our priorities change. *(change from being children to being adults),*

12. Students can be quite creative with the reasons they give for not **handing** .... their homework. *(giving their teachers)*

13. Salaries very rarely **keep** .... the cost of living. *(rise at the same speed as)*

14. The article is very detailed, but **leaves** .... the reasons for demographic change. *(does not include)*

15. The lecturer **pointed** .... all of the places on the map where similar incidents had occurred. *(showed)*

16. Before you write your essay, you should **look** .... the Party's history. *(research)*

17. Many employees **carried** .... working despite pressure from the unions. *(continued)*

18. Once people **fall** .... with their mortgage payments, they come under extreme financial pressure from their bank. *(become late)*

19. The first step to a healthier lifestyle is to **cut** .... amount of salt you consume. *(reduce)*

20. It is becoming more common for people to **cut** .... meat from their diet. *(stop eating)*

21. In the late 1990s, a lot of large supermarket chains **took** .... premises that had previously been run by small, independent retailers. *(assumed control)*

22. When computer technology fails us, we have to **make do** .... more primitive methods. They're called 'pen and paper'. *(use something because there is nothing else available)*

23. In this essay, I'd like to **put** .... the arguments for and against globalism. *(suggest or state the case for something)*

24. When I **look** .... my childhood, I remember the many sacrifices my parents made for me. *(think about something that happened in the past)*

Complete the second sentence in each pair with a phrasal verb from the box so that it has the same meaning as the first sentence. You will need to change the verb form in many of the sentences.

break down	carry out	cut back on	cut off	do away with	do up
end up	fall through	hold up	keep on	let down	let off
pull out of	pull through	show up	sort out	split up	wear off
wear out	work out				

1. Peace talks between the two countries collapsed when neither side reached an agreement.

   Peace talks between the two countries .... when neither side reached an agreement.

2. I'm trying to calculate if we've sold more this year than last year.

   I'm trying to .... if we've sold more this year than last year.

3. The effects of the drug disappear after a few hours.

   The effects of the drug .... after a few hours.

4. A lot of people exhaust themselves through overwork.

   A lot of people .... themselves .... through overwork.

5. Despite the severity of the disease, many people recover with the help of appropriate drugs.

   Despite the severity of the disease, many people .... with the help of appropriate drugs.

6. Through careful negotiation, they were able to resolve the problem.

   Through careful negotiation, they were able to .... the problem.

7. When parents start to live apart, it can be particularly difficult for their children to cope.

   When parents .... , it can be particularly difficult for their children to cope.

8. At the opening night, only a few audience members came.

   At the opening night, only a few audience members ....

9. The Australian partners stopped being a part of the deal at the last moment.

   The Australian partners .... the deal at the last moment.

10. People celebrate the Chinese New Year by exploding fireworks in the street.

    People celebrate the Chinese New Year by .... fireworks in the street.

Phrasal verbs 2

11. It is pointless relying on people to help you if they don't do as they promised.

It is pointless relying on people to help you if they .... you ....

12. New government pension plans mean that many people will continue working well into their seventies.

New government pension plans mean that many people will .... working well into their seventies.

13. The planned changes were delayed because committee members argued among themselves.

The planned changes were .... because committee members argued among themselves.

14. At the last minute, the plans for the proposed motorway didn't take place.

At the last minute, the plans for the proposed motorway ....

15. During the recession, many workers in the primary sector became jobless.

During the recession, many workers in the primary sector .... jobless.

16. Doctors did some tests on the patients.

Doctors .... some tests on the patients.

17. Minor economies, such as spending less on staff costs, can often prevent a company sliding into bankruptcy.

Minor economies, such as .... staff costs, can often prevent a company sliding into bankruptcy.

18. We were accidentally disconnected in the middle of our phone call.

We were accidentally .... in the middle of our phone call.

19. Once the government removed quotas, the market was flooded with cheap foreign imports.

Once the government .... quotas, the market was flooded with cheap foreign imports.

20. It cost almost £8 million to renovate the stadium, by which time the team was in serious financial difficulties.

It cost almost £8 million to .... the stadium, by which time the team was in serious financial difficulties.

Phrasal verbs 3

Complete these sentences with *come, get, give, go* or *look* to make a phrasal verb with the preposition or particle in bold. Make sure you use the correct form of the verb in each one.

1. I loved school as a child, and never really *looked* **forward to** the holidays as much as the other children.

2. In rural districts, it can be difficult to .... **by** without a car.

3. The 'drive safely' message is finally .... **through to** people, and there are now fewer accidents on the roads.

4. After years of decline, government investment is revitalising the area, and things are finally .... **up** for local businesses.

5. As ticket prices .... **up**, fewer people go to the cinema, preferring instead to stay at home and do other things.

6. I believe that people who have to .... **after** elderly relatives or other dependants should receive financial support.

7. Large companies can no longer .... **away with** dumping industrial waste in rivers.

8. Even if you fail the first time, you should .... **on** trying.

9. Scientists .... **across** the cure by accident while they were studying the health benefits of a rare tropical plant.

10. The first step to a healthier lifestyle is to .... **up** smoking.

11. Although many children .... **up to** their parents, many rebel against their values and way of life.

12. People who want to know how to .... **about** starting up their own website should read *Websites Made Easy*.

13. The gas fire heating the container............... **out**, and the apparatus started to cool down rapidly.

14. We decided not to .... **through** with our plans until we had made enough money.

15. Some people tend to .... **down on** those who are less fortunate than they are.

16. Wealthy countries are usually able to .... **through** a period of recession by drawing on financial reserves.

17. In any dispute with a major company, it is usually the customer who .... **off** the worst.

18. Before I handed my essay in, I .... **through** it very carefully, checking for mistakes.

19. People who live in close proximity to one another must try to .... **on with** their neighbours.

20. When our local council tried to build a ring road around the town, they .... **up against** a lot of opposition.

Phrasal verbs 4

The verbs and particles in the two boxes can be combined to make phrasal verbs, which can then be used to complete the sentences below.

Decide which phrasal verbs go into each sentence, and write the answers in the crossword grid. In many cases, you will need to change the form of the verb. The meaning of each phrasal verb is in *italics* at the end of each sentence.

Don't forget that some phrasal verbs need two particles.

The first one has been done as an example.

opt	make	pick	put	run
set	stand	take	talk	
turn				

after	against	aside	down
for	in	off	on	out
round	up	with	

Clues across (➔)

1. Accommodation in some cities is so expensive that some people cannot even afford to _____ the eight weeks' deposit that is required. *(to make a deposit)* **Answer = put down**

4. They were reluctant to make changes, but we managed to _____ them _____. *(to persuade somebody)*

5. Children often _____ one of their parents, either in their mannerisms or in the way they look. *(to resemble)*

6. After _____ a few unexpected difficulties, they decided to scrap the project. *(to stop because something is in the way)*

8. They were _____ of the apartment by their landlord when they could no longer afford the rent, and ended up living on the street. *(to be forced to leave)*

11. When I was at school, some teachers unfairly _____ children who avoided sport because they prefered more creative interests and pastimes. *(to choose someone to attack or criticise)*

12. Although many companies offer their employees a pension programme, many decide to _____ of the programme and make their own arrangements. *(to decide not to take part in something)*

16. A lot of applicants expressed an interest in the job, but only a handful _____ for the interview. *(to arrive for a meeting, appointment, etc.)*

19. Air pollution can _____ asthma and other chest diseases in those most vulnerable. *(to start)*

20. People who use credit cards unwisely can easily _____ debts of thousands of pounds every month. *(to make debts go up quickly)*

21. By the time he was 18, he had _____ his mind that he wanted to be famous. *(to decide on something)*

Clues down (⬇)

1. It's often a good idea to _____ some money for a 'rainy day'. *(to save money)*

2. Technology is moving at such a fast pace it is no longer possible to _____ all the latest developments. *(to understand or assimilate information)*

3. Nobody was _____ by the government's false figures on unemployment. *(to be fooled or tricked)*

5. He _____ the job that was offered to him, even though he was desperate for the money. *(to refuse something which is offered)*

7. Most people will _____ a stressful job if the money is good enough. *(to tolerate something which is not very pleasant)*

9. He was unable to make the speech, so I was asked to _____ and make it on his behalf. *(to take the place of someone – often also used with 'for')*

10. A lot of people are _____ the idea of working for themselves because of the lack of a regular salary. *(to be discouraged from doing something, usually because of a potentially negative outcome)*

13. Once bad weather _____, people tend to stay at home rather than go out. *(to start and become permanent)*

14. Doctors and medical experts were unable to _____ why some people survived the virus and others didn't. *(to understand or know the reason for something)*

15. She _____ a story about ghosts in the cellar to stop us going down there, but of course we didn't believe her. *(to invent a story)*

17. At the age of 38 he _____ the post of President, but lacked sufficient experience to be taken seriously. *(to apply for a job in politics, competing against other people for the same job)*

18. Despite massive promotion by the tourist board. it took a long time for tourism to _____ again after the terrorist attacks. *(to improve, to get better)*

Presenting an argument

Look at this typical IELTS Writing Test Part 2 question and the sample answer which follows it. Underline the most appropriate words and phrases in bold in the answer. In several cases, both options are possible.

Write about the following topic:

Some say that young people should take a break between school and university to go travelling and learn more about the world. Others say that it is better for them to go straight to university from school, and then go travelling when they have finished their studies.

Discuss both these views and give your own opinion.

Give reasons for your answer and include any relevant examples from your own knowledge and experience.

Write at least 250 words.

These days, it is very common for young people to take time off studying between school and university. Many of them go travelling, and spend a year or longer visiting interesting and exotic places. (1) **But / However,** is it better to do this, or to continue studying without a break?

(2) **First of all / Firstly,** there are several benefits to taking time off to travel.
(3) **As well as / In addition to** meeting lots of interesting people, you can also experience cultures that are very different from your own. (4) **I believe / I think** that first-hand knowledge and experience of the world around you early in life are useful things to have.
(5) **Moreover / Furthermore,** you learn to look after yourself in different and often difficult situations. (6) **Although / While** few people have serious problems when they travel, you will occasionally encounter situations where you need to think and act quickly without having friends or family to turn to. Unfortunately, travelling has its disadvantages (7) **also / as well,** such as homesickness and culture shock. (8) **Despite / Nevertheless,** these inconveniences are an inevitable part of travelling and are greatly outweighed by the advantages.

(9) **The most important reason / The main reason** for going straight to university after school is the fact that the sooner you get qualifications, the quicker you can get a job and start earning.
(10) **As far as I am concerned / For me,** starting work and making money is one of the most important things in life. I am not alone in this opinion. (11) **Many consider / Many say** a sound career and a good salary to be one of life's most important goals. (12) **Second / Secondly,** if you go straight to university, you learn so many things that will help you in your future life.
(13) **Eventually / Finally,** going straight to university from school means that you maintain a momentum that you might lose if you go travelling. (14) **I mean / In other words,** you remain focused on studying.

(15) **In conclusion / To summarise,** I would say that spending a year travelling between school and university has its advantages and disadvantages. (16) **On the one hand / To begin,** you are seeing something of the world. (17) **After that / On the other hand,** you are delaying your education and career. (18) **In my opinion / I opinion that,** it is better to carry on with your studies, and leave the travelling until later.

Reason & result

1 Join the first part of a sentence in the left-hand column with a second part from the right-hand column, using an appropriate word or phrase showing reason or result from the central column. In some cases, more than one answer is possible.

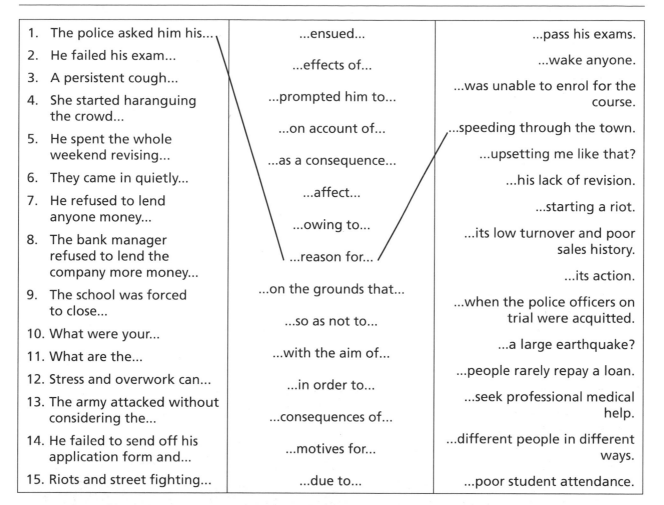

1. The police asked him his...	...ensued...	...pass his exams.
2. He failed his exam...	...effects of...	...wake anyone.
3. A persistent cough...	...prompted him to...	...was unable to enrol for the course.
4. She started haranguing the crowd...	...on account of...	...speeding through the town.
5. He spent the whole weekend revising...	...as a consequence...	...upsetting me like that?
6. They came in quietly...	...affect...	...his lack of revision.
7. He refused to lend anyone money...	...owing to...	...starting a riot.
8. The bank manager refused to lend the company more money...	...reason for...	...its low turnover and poor sales history.
9. The school was forced to close...	...on the grounds that...	...its action.
10. What were your...	...so as not to...	...when the police officers on trial were acquitted.
11. What are the...	...with the aim of...	...a large earthquake?
12. Stress and overwork can...	...in order to...	...people rarely repay a loan.
13. The army attacked without considering the...	...consequences of...	...seek professional medical help.
14. He failed to send off his application form and...	...motives for...	...different people in different ways.
15. Riots and street fighting...	...due to...	...poor student attendance.

2 Now complete these sentences with an appropriate word or phrase from the central column of the table above.

1. Panic buying .... when the stock market crashed.

2. People often do things without considering the .... their actions.

3. The government raised the income tax rate .... curb inflation.

4. The government raised the income tax rate .... curbing inflation.

5. The government raised the income tax rate .... the rapidly rising rate of inflation.

6. When questioned, many racists cannot give a logical .... their attitudes towards other racial groups.

7. The soaring crime rate alarmed the police superintendent and .... adopt a zero-tolerance policing policy.

8. He was arrested .... he was a danger to others and himself.

9. The family was forced to economise .... go heavily into debt.

10. The fumes from motor traffic .... people in many different ways.

Shape & features

1 (Shape) Match the words in the box with the shapes. Write the word next to each shape.

| a crescent | a circle | a cone | a cube | a cylinder | an oval | a pyramid |
| a rectangle | a sphere | a spiral | a square | a triangle | | |

1. .... 2. .... 3. .... 4. .... 5. .... 6. ....

7. .... 8. .... 9. .... 10. .... 11. .... 12. ....

2 (Shape) Complete the crossword with the adjective form of these shapes.

1. a circle
2. a rectangle
3. an oval
4. a spiral
5. a sphere
6. a triangle
7. a cone
8. a cylinder
9. a square

3 (Features) Match the descriptions 1 – 10 on the left with the objects, geographical features, etc (a) – (j) on the right. Use your dictionary to check the meanings of the words in bold.

1. **Sharp**, with **jagged** teeth
2. **Steep**, with a **pointed** peak.
3. **Rolling**, with **undulating** wheat fields.
4. **Curved**, with a **smooth** surface.
5. **Thin** and **flat**, with words and **dotted** lines.
6. **Wavy**, with a few **spiky** bits sticking up.
7. **Meandering**, with a **calm** surface.
8. **Winding** and **bumpy**, with **deep** potholes.
9. **Hollow**, with a **rough** surface.
10. **Thick**, **solid** and **heavy**, with **straight** edges.

(a) A country road in very poor condition.
(b) Somebody's hair.
(c) A very old tree.
(d) A knife.
(e) A slow-moving river.
(f) A brick.
(g) A mountain.
(h) A banana.
(i) Agricultural countryside.
(j) An application form.

Size, quantity & dimension

1 Look at the following list and decide whether we are talking about something *big* (in terms of size, quantity or dimension) or something *small*. <u>Underline</u> your answers

1. a *minute* amount of dust **Big** / <u>**Small**</u>

2. a *minuscule* piece of cloth **Big** / **Small**

3. an *enormous* book **Big** / **Small**

4. a *mammoth* job **Big** / **Small**

5. a *huge* waste of time **Big** / **Small**

6. a *vast* room **Big** / **Small**

7. a *gigantic* wave **Big** / **Small**

8. a *tiny* car **Big** / **Small**

9. a *monumental* error **Big** / **Small**

10. a *colossal* statue **Big** / **Small**

11. *plenty* of food **Big** / **Small**

12. *loads* of times **Big** / **Small**

13. a *narrow* alleyway **Big** / **Small**

14. a *giant* building **Big** / **Small**

15. a *gargantuan* meal **Big** / **Small**

16. a *wide* avenue **Big** / **Small**

17. a *broad* river **Big** / **Small**

18. a *tall* man **Big** / **Small**

19. a *high* mountain **Big** / **Small**

20. a *deep* lake **Big** / **Small**

21. a *shallow* pool **Big** / **Small**

22. a *long-distance* journey **Big** / **Small**

23. a *vast* crowd of supporters **Big** / **Small**

24. *tons* of work **Big** / **Small**

25. a *great deal of* time **Big** / **Small**

2 Now complete these sentences using one of the expressions above. In some cases, more than one answer is possible.

1. Before you embark on .... , it is essential that you are well prepared.

2. We spent .... working on the plans for the new library.

3. I love the Museum of Modern Art, and have been there ....

4. There's a small grey spot in the corner of all my photographs, so I guess .... must have got into the camera and ended up on the sensor.

5. Villages along the coast were destroyed when .... caused by the earthquake swept houses into the sea.

6. In my opinion, playing computer games for hours on end is ....

7. .... of the Greek god Poseidon stood by the entrance to the harbour.

Size, quantity & dimension

8. Despite the poor harvest, there was .... for the whole population.

9. .... called the Thames separates the city of London from the suburbs to the south.

10. .... gathered to see their favourite football team.

11. We ate .... and then lay down to rest.

12. The most impressive place in the building is .... called the Great Hall, which can hold over 3,000 people.

13. We have .... to do in the next few days, so I suggest we start as soon as possible.

14. Loch Ness is .... in the Highlands of Scotland.

15. The only evidence of the crime was .... which was stuck on a branch of one of the trees in the garden.

16. 'Sumo' is .... containing almost 1,000 pictures by the controversial photographer Helmut Newton.

17. I had .... to do, so took the phone off the hook, made myself some coffee and sat down at my desk.

18. The Matterhorn, ... in Switzerland, has claimed the lives of many who have tried to climb it.

19. He made .... in his calculations and had to start all over again.

20. The manufacturers have built .... which is ideal for getting around the city.

21. The NEC in Birmingham is .... which is used for concerts and exhibitions.

22. The main feature of the town is .... lined with shops and cafés.

23. I could see the key glittering at the bottom of ....

24. Early European settlers in Central and South America heard legends of .... called El Dorado who covered himself in gold dust.

25. .... ran along the side of the house to a garden at the rear.

Spelling

Each passage below contains 12 words which have been spelt incorrectly. <u>Underline</u> the words, then write their correct spelling in the box below.

1

Despite banning tobacco <u>advertiseing</u> and rising the price of cigarrettes, the goverment's anti-smoking campain has failed to have any long-term affects. It is now widely beleived that more drastic measures are neccessary. A new national comittee, which has been formed to tackle the proplem, has made several reccomendations. These include banning smoking in all public areas, and denying hospital treatment to persistant smokers who have been warned by their doctors to give up but failed to do so.

advertising			

2

It is <u>argueable</u> wether good pronounciation is more important than good grammer and vocabulery. Consientious students balance their aquisition of these skills, hopeing to acheive both fluency and accuracey. English teachers should encourage there students to practise all the relevant language skills, and use their English at every oportunity.

arguable			

3

It is <u>becomming</u> increasingly dificult for many people to find decent accomodation in the city at a price they can afford. To put it simpley, there are to many people and not enough homes for them. Local comunity centres and charitable organiseations such as *Home Front* can offer advise, but it is widely agreed that the situation is no longer managable. The fact that some councils in the city are building cheap, tempory housing for lower-paid profesionals is the only official acknowlegement of this problem.

becomming			

Stopping something

Choose the best word or phrase in bold to complete each sentence, using the definitions in *italics* after each sentence to help you.

1. To stop your hard disk becoming too full, you should **delete / dissuade / sever** any unwanted programmes. (*to cut out part of a document, a computer file, etc.*)

2. The new government plans to **back out of / repeal / suppress** the existing legislation. (*to officially end a law so that it is no longer valid*)

3. Increasing fuel prices does not usually **deter / quash / rescind** people from using their cars. (*to discourage people from doing something*)

4. The college tries to **cancel / dissuade / give up** students from taking exams which are not suitable for them. (*to persuade someone not to do something*)

5. The committee decided to **deny / remove / rescind** its earlier resolution on the use of its premises. (*to cancel a contract or agreement*)

6. State monopolies often **back out of / suppress / suspend** all forms of economic competition. (*to stop an activity, usually by making laws or using your authority*)

7. The Cornucopian government made the sudden decision to **dissuade / rescind / sever** diplomatic relations with their neighbouring countries. (*to end something such as a friendship or a connection completely and permanently*)

8. You should never **deny / put an end to / turn down** a good job when it's offered to you. (*to refuse something which is offered*)

9. We decided to **pull out of / remove / rescind** the competition when three of our team members became ill. (*to decide not to support or be part of a project or activity after you have agreed to*)

10. Oil and petroleum companies **deny / scrap / repeal** that they are harming the environment. (*to state that something someone has said is not true or correct*)

11. Travel companies do not normally give refunds if their customers **cancel / put an end to / sever** their holiday at the last moment. (*to stop something which has been planned*)

12. It's important to **deter / remove / quash** rumours before too many people hear them. (*to stop something from continuing, especially things people say or believe: rumours, doubts, speculation, etc.*)

13. You should **delete / give up / suppress** fast food and other foods that have a high fat content if you want to lose weight. (*to stop doing something that you have done for quite a long time*)

14. They finally agreed to **dissuade / put an end to / quash** their long-standing dispute and try to work together instead. (*to stop something which has been going on for a long time*)

15. I would be grateful if you would **deter / remove / repeal** my name from your mailing list. (*to take something away*)

16. The factory management had to **deny / suspend / turn down** operations because of some serious health and safety issues. (*to officially stop something for a short time*)

17. We were forced to **give up / rescind / scrap** the plans when we realised they would not work. (*to decide not to continue with something such as a plan or event, often because there is a problem with some aspect of it*)

18. I believe that the best way to **delete / curb / repeal** inflation is to increase interest rates on borrowing. (*to control or limit something that is harmful*)

Success & failure

Arrange the letters in bold to make verbs and phrases connected with success and failure. The first letter is in its correct place, and the words you need can be found in the grid at the bottom of the page by reading horizontally across (⇨) or vertically down (⇩).

Success

1. The two departments **radheec** a compromise over how to proceed with the project. _reached_

2. During his first month as head of the company, he was able to **aospclimch** more than his predecessor had in the previous six. ....

3. Our team played well and **scerdeu** their second win of the season. ....

4. The first signs that a breakthrough had been **aicehdve** quickly became apparent. ....

5. Many people want to be rich and famous, but very few **rlesaie** their dream. ....

6. Becoming an Olympic athlete requires hard work and dedication, but few athletes **aatnit** the required standard of physical excellence. ....

7. His journey up the Amazon **flfludlei** a long-cherished ambition. ....

8. After several attempts, we **mndagea** to solve the problem. ....

Failure

9. They had to **aadbnno** their idea of travelling by boat, and flew instead. ....

10. Negotiations **claedpsol** when neither side could agree on the terms and conditions. ....

11. Progress on the research project **fraledte** when the money began to run out. ....

12. After a disastrous year, the company **fdoedl**, with debts of over £2 million. ....

13. Our planned visit to Sudan **flle turohhg** when we were unable to get visas. ....

14. The company's plans to double prices **mefdiris** when the government declared their actions illegal. ....

F	U	L	F	I	L	L	E	D	Q	F	W
R	T	R	A	B	A	N	D	O	N	O	E
U	S	E	C	U	R	E	D	I	O	L	C
R	E	A	C	H	E	D	P	A	S	D	O
D	F	L	O	G	H	J	L	K	X	E	L
A	Z	I	M	I	S	F	I	R	E	D	L
T	C	S	P	V	B	N	M	K	D	R	A
T	T	E	L	M	A	N	A	G	E	D	P
A	C	H	I	E	V	E	D	K	P	O	S
I	S	T	S	Y	J	F	E	H	U	H	E
N	A	R	H	F	A	L	T	E	R	E	D
F	E	L	L	T	H	R	O	U	G	H	Z

Task commands

1 Look at the list of tasks in sentences 1 – 8. In particular, look at the words and phrases in bold, which are telling the writer / speaker what he / she must do. Match these words with a suitable definition of the task command in A – H.

1. **Account for** the increased use of social networking on the Internet. ....*F*....

2. **Analyse** the effects of climate change around the world. ....

3. **Evaluate** the improvements you have made to your English since you started using this book. ....

4. **Compare** and **contrast** the two machines. ....

5. **Define** 'happiness', and say how important it is. ....

6. **Demonstrate** the different features on this mobile phone. ....

7. **Discuss** the advantages and disadvantages of growing up in a big city. ....

8. **Elaborate on** your feelings about global capitalism. ....

A. Give the meaning of something.

B. Talk about something with someone else, or write about it from different viewpoints.

C. Calculate the value, importance or effect of something.

D. Explain something closely and scientifically.

E. Explain something in more detail than you did previously.

F. Say why something has happened or is happening.

G. Show how something works, usually by physically operating it so that the other person knows what it does and how it works.

H. Look at two things side by side to see in what way they are similar and / or different.

2 Now do the same with these.

1. **Estimate** the costs of setting up a website for the school. ....

2. **Examine** the causes of global warming. ....

3. **Illustrate** the problems caused by the increased use of private vehicles. ....

4. **Justify** your reasons for only considering one aspect of the problem. ....

5. **Outline** your country's environmental policy. ....

6. **Predict** the changes that we are going to see in information technology in the next 10 years. ....

7. **Suggest** ways in which food shortages in some countries could be solved. ....

8. **Trace** the development of space travel since the 1960s. ....

A. Explain, with real examples, why something has happened or is happening.

B. Say what you think is going to happen in the future.

C. Describe what you think can be done in order to achieve something.

D. Calculate (but not exactly) the value or cost of something.

E. Give the main points of something, or a broad description of something, without giving too much detail.

F. Give a brief history of something, in the order in which it happened.

G. Write or talk about the different aspects (e.g., causes, results) of something.

H. Show that you have a good reason for doing something, especially if other people think you have done something wrong or bad.

1 Use the words and phrases in the boxes to complete the sentences. Pay particular attention to the words that come before or after the words and phrases.

Part 1: One action or situation occurring before another action or situation

| by the time | earlier | formerly | precede | previously | prior to |

1. ....the advent of the Industrial Revolution, pollution was virtually unheard of.
2. ....the army had restored order, the city had been almost completely devastated.
3. ....known as Bombay, Mumbai is India's most vibrant and exciting city.
4. A sudden drop in temperature will usually ....a blizzard.
5. It was my first trip on an aeroplane. ....I'd always gone by train.
6. The Prime Minister made a speech praising charity organisations working in Mozambique. ....that day he had promised massive economic aid to stricken areas.

Part 2: One action or situation occurring at the same time as another action or situation

| at that very moment | during | in the meantime | while |

1. ....the minister was making his speech, thousands of demonstrators took to the streets.
2. .... the speech they jeered and shouted slogans.
3. The minister continued speaking. .... the police were ordered onto the streets.
4. He finished the speech with a word of praise for the police. .... people began throwing bottles and bricks, and the riot began.

Part 3: One action or situation occurring after another action or situation

| afterwards | as soon as | following |

1. .... the earthquake, emergency organisations around the world swung into action.
2. .... the stock market collapsed, there was panic buying on an unprecedented scale.
3. The Klondike gold rush lasted from 1896 to 1910. ...., the area became practically deserted overnight.

2 Look at these words and phrases and decide if we usually use them to talk about (1) the past, (2) the past leading to the present, (3) the present or (4) the future. Try to write a sentence for each one.

| a few decades ago   as things stand   at the turn of the century
at that point / moment in history   back in the 1990s   between 2003 and 2005
by the end of this year   ever since   for the foreseeable future
for the next few weeks   for the past few months   from 2006 to 2011
from now on   in another five years' time   in medieval times
in my childhood / youth   in those days   last century   lately   nowadays
one day   over the coming weeks and months   over the past six weeks
sooner or later   these days |

Useful interview expressions

1 Here are some common spoken expressions that you might find useful in the IELTS Speaking Test. Put each expression into the correct box in the table according to its function.

1. ~~Could I just say that...~~
2. What are your views on...?
3. ~~Do you agree that...?~~
4. Sorry to interrupt,...
5. Excuse me for interrupting,...
6. ~~I agree.~~
7. Well, as a matter of fact,...
8. I couldn't agree more.
9. That's my view exactly.
10. What are your feelings about...?

11. ~~I don't entirely agree.~~
12. I see things rather differently myself.
13. Let me interrupt you there.
14. What do you think about...?
15. Sorry to butt in,...
16. That's just what I think.
17. That's right.
18. Well, actually,...
19. What's your opinion?
20. I'm afraid I disagree / don't agree.

Agreeing with somebody
I agree. ....
....
....
....
....

Disagreeing with somebody
I don't entirely agree. ....
....
....
....
....

Interrupting somebody
Could I just say that...? ....
....
....
....
....

Asking somebody for their opinion
Do you agree that...? ....
....
....
....
....

2 Now do the same with these.

1. ~~In other words,...~~
2. What I mean is...
3. May I think about that for a moment?
4. So, in conclusion,...
5. ~~Could you repeat the question?~~
6. Perhaps I should make that clearer by saying...
7. Let me see.
8. In short / brief,...
9. To sum up,...
10. I'm afraid I didn't catch that.

11. I'm sorry?
12. To put it another way...
13. Let me think about that for a moment.
14. That's an interesting question.
15. To summarise,...
16. What was that?
17. What I'm trying to say is...
18. ~~Hmm, how can I put / say this?~~
19. ~~So, basically,...~~
20. Would you mind repeating that?

Useful interview expressions

Asking for clarification or repetition
Could you repeat the question? ....
....
....
....
....

Saying something in another way
In other words... ....
....
....
....
....

Giving yourself time to think
Hmm, how can I put / say this? ....
....
....
....
....

Summing up what you have said
So, basically... ....
....
....
....
....

3 Fill in the gaps in these extracts from IELTS-style interviews with a suitable expression from Exercise 1 or 2. In each case, more than one answer is possible.

1.
Interviewer: Why are so many people obsessed with celebrities?
Student: ....
Interviewer: Why are so many people obsessed with celebrities?

2.
Interviewer: A lot of people say that we've become too reliant on technology. What's your opinion?
Student: .... In fact, I think that it's taking over our lives.

3.
Interviewer: Do you think that people in places like India, Bangladesh and other African countries work harder...
Student: .... but don't you mean *Asian* countries?
Interviewer: Of course, yes, that's what I meant.

4.
Interviewer: Some professional sports people are paid far too much. Do you agree?
Student: .... First of all, I think that there are times when the salary they're paid is justified, but then again, a lot of them...

5.
Interviewer: The way parents behave can have a profound effect on how their children develop. Do you agree?
Student: Yes I do. Children need people who can influence them in a positive way, and who can show them the difference between right and wrong. .... they need good role models.

6.
Interviewer: Some people say that private vehicle ownership should be banned, and we should all use public transport. Are they right, do you think?
Student: .... First of all, public transport can't always take you exactly where you want to go. Secondly, it's expensive and unreliable. Then there's the problem with....

Architecture

1 Put the words and phrases in the box into their appropriate category in the table beneath. Some words or phrases can go into more than one category. The material in this module basically remains the same, with the exception of the following changes:

art deco   concrete   controversial   elegant   energy-efficient
an eyesore   façade   foundations   functional   glass
high-rise apartments   high-tech   international style
low-rise apartments   modernist   multi-storey car park   post-modern
pleasing geometric forms   porch   practical   reinforced concrete
skyscraper   standardised   steel   stone   timber   traditional   ugly
walls   well-designed

Building materials (6 words / phrases)	Aesthetic perception (how we feel about a building) (6 words / phrases)

Types of building (4 words / phrases)	Architectural style (6 words / phrases)

Parts of a building (4 words / phrases)	Features (that make the building easy to live or work in) (4 words / phrases)

2 Complete these sentences with an appropriate word or phrase from A, B or C.

1. The building is .... It's been ruined and abandoned for years.

   A. destabilised   **B. derelict**   **C. defunct**

2. She lives on a large housing .... near the centre of the city.

   A. estate   **B. state**   **C. estuary**

3. There are several run-down districts inside the city where the housing is in a bad state, although most of these .... are going to be replaced by high-rise apartments.

   A. slumps   **B. scrums**   **C. slums**

4. The city council are going to .... the old church and built a new one in its place.

   A. demobilise   **B. demote**   **C. demolish**

5. You can't knock down that house; there's a .... order on it which makes it illegal to destroy it.

   A. preservation   **B. preservative**   **C. presentable**

6. Sir Richard Rogers is the .... who designed the Lloyds building in London.

   A. architect   **B. architecture**   **C. architectural**

7. Some of the problems in our .... are drug related.

   A. inter-cities   **B. internal cities**   **C. inner cities**

8. The council hope to reduce crime in the town by introducing new .... facilities so that people have something to do in the evening.

   A. sociable   **B. socialist**   **C. social**

9. The cinema is going to be closed for two months while the owners .... it.

   A. renovate   **B. remonstrate**   **C. reiterate**

10. If you want to add an extension to your house, you will need .... permission from your local council.

    A. planning   **B. construction**   **C. plotting**

11. In the US, the ground floor is called the .... floor.

    A. basement   **B. first**   **C. bottom**

12. One way of creating more space in a house is to convert the .... into an extra room.

    A. attic   **B. ceiling**   **C. roof**

Architecture

3 Complete this report with words and phrases from Exercises 1 and 2. In some cases, more than one answer is possible, and you will need to change the form of one of the words.

Report from the director of the West Twyford Town Planning Committee

The last year has been a busy one for the West Twyford Town Planning Committee. Outlined below are a few of the areas we have concentrated on.

1. Applications for 1.. permission from home owners who want to develop their properties have increased by 50 per cent. However, many of these homes are historic buildings and have 2.. orders which prevent them from being altered externally. At present, we can only allow owners to 3.. the inside of their homes (including installing central heating and improved wall insulation).

2. Last summer we invited several 4.. to design plans for the new council offices on Peach Street. We eventually chose Barnard, Jackson and Willis, a local company. It was generally agreed that their design, which included a grey tinted 5.. 6.. at the front of the building, was the most aesthetically pleasing. They are currently in the process of laying the 7.. for the new building, which we understand is taking some time as the land must be drained first.

3. In response to a lot of complaints about the lack of 8.. facilities in the town, it was agreed at last month's meeting that funds should be set aside for the construction of a new sports centre and youth club.

4. Several 9.. buildings which have been ruined and abandoned for over five years are to be knocked down. In their place, a new housing 10.. will be built. This will provide 20 new homes within the next two years.

5. Everybody agrees that the new shops on the High Street are 11.. . It is certainly true that they are very ugly and out of keeping with the other buildings on the street. In future, we must ensure that all new buildings are built in a 12.. style so that they fit in with the older buildings around them.

6. There has been an increased crime rate in the 13.. to the east of the town. We plan to demolish these run-down areas within the next eight years and re-house the residents in new 14.. apartments in the Berkely Heath district.

7. In an attempt to help the environment, we are going to make the town hall more 15.. Windows will be double-glazed, walls and ceilings will be insulated and we will replace the current central heating system.

My next report will be in two months' time. Anybody wishing to discuss these issues can contact me on extension 287.

The arts

1 Look at the extracts from newspaper reviews, and decide what is being talked about in each one. Choose your answers from the box.

Fine / Visual arts

abstract art   a landscape   photography   a portrait   a sculpture
a still life

Literature

an autobiography   a biography   a collection of short stories   drama
a novel   poetry

Performing arts

a ballet   a concert   a film   a modern dance piece   a musical
an opera   a play

---

1. Mimi Latouche is getting a little too old for this kind of thing, and as I watched her pirouette across the stage in a tutu two sizes too small, she reminded me not so much of a swan as a rather ungainly crow. ....

2. The scenery was wonderful. The costumes were marvellous. The cast were incredible. I wish I could say the same about the script. The playwright should be shot. ....

3. In his new book on Ernest Hemingway, acclaimed writer Michael Norris has brought the great man to life in a way nobody else could. ....

4. Move over Michelangelo! You have a rival. Vittorio Manelleto's marble pieces embody the human form in a way that has not been achieved in over 500 years. ....

5. I had to study the picture for almost two minutes before I realised who it was. It was none other than our Queen. I doubt she would have been amused. ....

6. There are no great tenors in Britain. That is until now. Brian Clack's performance in *La Traviatta* sent shudders down my spine. What a man! What a voice! What a size! ....

7. Herbert von Erding has been conducting now for almost 40 years, and his final appearance yesterday was greeted with a standing ovation from both musicians and members of the audience. ....

8. *Stone Angel* is an hilarious tale about the fall and rise of an opera singer. I picked it up and didn't put it down until I had finished. A fantastic book. ....

9. Dylan Thomas showed remarkable eloquence, and this latest compilation of some of his finest prose will surely be a bestseller. ....

10. Bruschetta's studies of dead animals might not be to everyone's taste, but it is impossible to deny his skill in representing inanimate objects like these on canvas. ....

11. He usually works in black and white, and in my opinion that's the medium he should stick to. His colour shots are too static and are heavily over-filtered, the strong lighting washes out any subtlety, and much of it is out of focus. ....

The arts

12. Shot entirely on location in Iran, this is perhaps the director's finest hour. A stunning setting, fine performances from the leads, and a cast of thousands of extras make this a truly visual feast. ....

13. The painting shows a lot of red circles and triangles inside squares floating in the sky above a yellow sea, and is titled 'Contractual Obligation Metamorphosis'. ....

14. 'Dawn View of London' takes in the whole of the city as seen from the top of Parliament Hill, although the artist has removed some of the less attractive buildings from the foreground. ....

2 The words in bold in these sentences are either wrong, or the wrong word form has been used. Change them so that they are correct.

1. Tonight's **perform** of *Romeo and Juliet* begins at 7.30.   *performance*

2. Camford University Press have just released a collection of Shakespeare's **workings**. ....

3. A new limited **editor** of the CD 'Here we go!' by rock group Glass Weasel contains a DVD of their latest tour. ....

4. His last book received some excellent **revues** in the papers. ....

5. Tate Modern is currently running an **exhibit** of Tracey Emin's early work. ....

6. The British National Opera says that it is delighted with the government's promise of a £500,000 **granting**. ....

7. Tickets have already sold out for the first day's showing of Tom Cartmill's paintings at the National Art **Galley**. ....

8. Ernest Hemingway was one of the twentieth century's most famous **novels**. ....

9. French **impressionism**, which included Money, Manet and Degas, had a profound influence on nineteenth-century art. ....

10. Apparently, Oldhaven Press are going to **publication** a collection of short stories written by schoolchildren. ....

11. I loved the film's **atmosphere** music and use of visual metaphor. ....

12. I've always had an **arty** eye, and think I would make a good fashion photographer. ....

13. I hate reality shows, talent shows and similar television programmes that form the bulk of today's **popularity** culture. ....

14. Orson Welles' film *Citizen Kane* was made over 70 years ago, but remains a **cinema** masterpiece. ....

15. André Breton is widely regarded as the founder of the **surreal** art movement. ....

16. The college runs a varied programme of **cultured** activities which are open to ordinary members of the public. ....

3 Complete this extract from a radio programme with the words or phrases from Exercises 1 and 2. In some cases, more than one answer is possible, and you will need to change some of the word forms.

Hello, and welcome to today's edition of 'But is it Art?'

Now, I don't usually enjoy 1... – all those pirouettes and pas de deux's and dying swans usually send me to sleep, but last night's 2.. of *Sleeping Beauty* at Nureyev Hall had me on the edge of my seat. And I'm not the only one: rave 3.. in the national press praised the excellent choreography and the incredible stage set. It's on again tonight, but you'll have to move fast if you want a ticket!

The current 4.. of Monetto's paintings at the Wheatley Art 5.. has been a disappointment. The pictures themselves are excellent, especially the great artist's 6.. of film stars, and of course his stunning 7.. of a vase of daffodils, but the lighting inside the room was terrible. I would have thought that, having received a government 8.. of almost £100,000, the Wheatley Arts Council could have invested it in some good lights.

Fans of the great twentieth-century 9.. George Orwell will be delighted to hear that Swansong Press are going to release a collection of his greatest 10.. , which will of course include *Animal Farm* and *Nineteen Eighty Four*. Also included are some rare short stories which were not 11.. until after his death. Look out for the book, which will be in the shops from the end of the month.

On the subject of books, a new 12.. of the life of conductor Charles Worsenmost is due to be released in January. Worsenmost conducted his last 13.. in 1998 after a long and eventful career. This is highly recommended for anyone who is remotely interested in classical music.

Have you ever wanted to be an 14.. singer? Well, now's your chance! The National Music Company are looking for tenors and sopranos to audition for a new production of Mozart's *Marriage of Figaro*. If you're interested, we'll give you the number to call at the end of the programme.

Potential Michelangelos and Henry Moores can try their hand at 15.. this weekend. The Gleneagles Museum is holding a series of workshops which will give you the chance to chip away at a lump of stone to produce a piece of three-dimensional art. There's no need to book – just turn up at the door on Saturday at nine o'clock.

And now here's that number I promised you... .

Business & industry

1 Look at sentences 1 – 16, and replace the words and phrases in bold with a word or phrase in the box which has an opposite meaning.

credit   demand for   employees   expenditure   exports   lending
loss   net   private   recession   retail   shop floor
state-owned industries   take on   unskilled labourers   white-collar

1. We have a limited **supply of** computer base units.

2. Last year, our company made a huge **profit**.

3. Our **gross** profits are up by almost 150 per cent on last year.

4. Banks across the country are reporting a sharp drop in **borrowing**.

5. The company will **debit** your bank account with £528 each month.

6. The **wholesale** market has experienced a downturn since the recession began.

7. The government is encouraging short-term investors to put their money into the **public** sector.

8. **Private enterprises** are under a lot of financial pressure.

9. **Skilled workers** are demanding a 15 per cent pay rise.

10. If this continues, we will have to **lay off** members of staff.

11. **Blue-collar** workers across the country are demanding improved working conditions.

12. He works for a company which **imports** camera equipment.

13. A lot of people have benefited from the recent **boom** in the electrical industry.

14. The **management** refuse to compromise on the quality of their products.

15. Overall **revenue** is down by almost 15 per cent.

16. A fight broke out in the **boardroom** over terms and conditions of employment. (Note: you will have to change the preposition *in* to *on*)

Business & industry

2 Match the words and phrases in the first box with a dictionary definition from the list A – R below.

1. automation	7. interest rates	13. output
2. unemployment	8. primary industry	14. income tax
3. inflation	9. secondary industries	15. VAT
4. balance of payments	10. service industries	16. deficit
5. taxation	11. nationalised industries	17. key industry
6. GNP	12. monopoly	18. salary

A. The percentage charged for borrowing money. (*The Bank of England has raised* ....)

B. Industries involved in the manufacture of goods. (................................... *rely on the ready supply of raw materials.*)

C. The value of goods and services paid for in a country, including income earned in other countries. (*Last year's* .... *was close to £25 billion.*)

D. The amount which a firm, machine or person produces. (*The factory has doubled its* .... *in the last six months.*)

E. Industries involved in the production of raw materials. (*Coal mining is an important* ....)

F. Installing machinery in place of workers (................................... *can be a mixed blessing – machines usually tend to be out of order when you need them most.*)

G. Industries which do not make products but offer a service such as banking, insurance and transport. (................................... *have become more important in the last decade.*)

H. The difference in value between a country's imports and exports. (*The government is trying to reduce the* .... *deficit.*)

I. The amount by which expenditure is more than receipts in a firm's or country's accounts. (*The company announced a two million pound* ....)

J. A system where one person or company supplies all of a product in one area without any competition. (*The state has a* .... *of the tobacco trade.*)

K. Industries which were once privately owned, but now belong to the state. (*Workers in* .... *are to get a 3 per cent pay rise.*)

L. Lack of work. (*The figures for* .... *are rising.*)

M. The action of imposing taxes. (*Money raised by* .... *pays for all government services.*)

N. The most important industries in a country. (*Oil is a* .... *which is essential to the country's economy.*)

O. A state in an economy where prices and wages are rising to keep pace with each other. (*The government is trying to keep* .... *down below 3 per cent.*)

P. A tax on money earned as wages or salary. (*She pays* .... *at the lowest rate.*)

Q. A tax imposed as a percentage of the invoice value of goods or services. An indirect tax. (................................... *in Britain currently runs at 20 per cent.*)

R. A fixed amount of money that you earn each month of year from your job (*I receive an annual* .... *of £30,000*)

Business & industry

3 Complete this extract from a business programme with words and phrases from Exercises 1 and 2. In some cases, more than one answer is possible, and you will need to change some of the word forms.

1.. rates are to rise by a further half a per cent next month, putting further pressure on homeowners paying mortgages. It will also discourage people from 2.. money from the high street banks, who are already under a lot of pressure. Last year, the National Bank was forced to 3.. 2,000 members of staff across the country, adding to the country's rapidly rising rate of 4.. .

5.. rose in the last year by almost 6 per cent, despite the government's pledge to keep price and wage rises no higher than 3 per cent. This has had a negative impact on 6.. , since the strong pound coupled with rising prices has made it almost impossible for foreign companies to buy British goods and services. Especially affected are the 7.. producing pharmaceuticals and chemicals.

8.. workers in 9.. industries across the country are demanding higher 10.. . Unions and workers are negotiating with 11.. chiefs for an eight percent rise. This follows the announcement that the government want more investors to put their money into the 12.. sector.

13.. for home computers has finally overtaken the 14.. , making it once again a seller's market. There is now a two-week waiting list to receive a new computer. This has pushed prices up by almost a third.

Bradford Aerospace Technologies, where overall 15.. for sales of aircraft parts has dropped by almost 10 per cent in the last quarter, will shortly become a 16.. industry in a final desperate attempt to keep it open. The government has promised it will keep on the current workforce.

Bad news too for Ranger Cars, who this week announced a 17.. of almost £5 million. A spokesman for the company blamed high labour costs and the reluctance by union leaders to approve increased 18.. at the firm's factories. They insist that the installation of new machinery will lead to redundancies.

Children & the family

1 Complete these sentences with an appropriate word or phrase from A, B or C.

1. Mr and Mrs Smith live at home with their two children. They are a typical example of a modern .... family.

    A. extended   **B. nuclear**   **C. compact**

2. Mr and Mrs Popatlal live at home with their aged parents, children and grandchildren. They are a typical example of a traditional .... family.

    A. nuclear   **B. enlarged**   **C. extended**

3. Mrs Jones lives on her own and has to look after her two children. There are a lot of .... families like hers.

    A. single-parent   **B. mother-only**   **C. mono-parent**

4. Some parents need to .... their children more strictly.

    A. bring down   **B. bring about**   **C. bring up**

5. When I was a child, I had a very turbulent ....

    A. upbringing   **B. upraising**   **C. uplifting**

6. Mrs Kelly is .... and finds it difficult to look after her children on her own.

    A. divorced   **B. divided**   **C. diverged**

7. Many men believe that .... is the responsibility of a woman.

    A. childhelp   **B. childcare**   **C. childaid**

8. .... is a particularly difficult time of life for a child.

    A. Convalescence   **B. Adolescence**   **C. Convergence**

9. A person's behaviour can sometimes be traced back to his/her ....

    A. creative years   **B. formulating years**   **C. formative years**

10. The country has seen a sharp drop in the .... in the last few years.

    A. birth rate   **B. baby rate**   **C. born rate**

11. She has five .... who rely on her to look after them.

    A. dependants   **B. dependers**   **C. dependents**

12. .... crime is on the rise, with over 30 per cent of thefts being committed by young people under the age of eighteen.

    A. Junior   **B. Juvenile**   **C. Children**

2 Match sentences 1 – 12 with a second sentence A – M. Use the key words and phrases in bold to help you.

1. Mr and Mrs White are very **authoritarian** parents.
2. Mr Bowles is considered to be too **lenient**.
3. Mr and Mrs Harris lead **separate lives**.
4. Billy is a **well-adjusted** kid.
5. The Mannings are not very **responsible** parents.
6. My parents are **separated**.
7. Parents must look after their children, but they shouldn't be **over-protective**.
8. Professor Maynard has made a study of the **cognitive processes** of young children.

Children & the family

9. I'm afraid my youngest child is **running wild**.

10. She looks quite different from all her **siblings**.

11. There are several **different and distinct stages of development** in a child's life.

12. Tony was raised by a **foster family** when his own parents died.

A. They don't look after their children very well.

B. He is fascinated by the way they learn new things.

C. He very rarely punishes his children.

D. I live with my mother and visit my father at weekends.

E. He never listens to a word I say, and is always playing truant from school.

F. Brothers and sisters usually bear some resemblance to one another.

G. Although they are married and live together, they rarely speak to each other.

H. They are very strict with their children.

I. Of all of these, the teenage years are the most difficult.

J. Children need the freedom to get out and experience the world around them.

K. He's happy at home and is doing well at school.

L. Many families take in children who are not their own.

3 Complete this case study with one of the words or phrases from Exercises 1 and 2. You will need to change one of the word forms.

Bob's problems began during his 1.. years. His parents got 2.. when he was young, and neither of them wanted to raise him or his brother and sister, so he was 3.. by a 4.. chosen by his parents' social worker. Unfortunately, his foster father was a strict 5.. and often beat him. Bob rebelled against this strict 6.. , and by the time he was eight, he was already 7.. , stealing from shops and playing truant. By the time he reached 8.. , sometime around his 13th birthday, he had already appeared in court several times, charged with 9.. crime. The judge blamed his foster parents, explaining that children needed 10.. parents and guardians who would look after them properly. The foster father objected to this, pointing out that Bob's 11.. – his two brothers and sister – were 12.. children who behaved at home and worked well at school.

This has raised some interesting questions about the modern family system. While it is true that parents should not be too 13.. with children by letting them do what they want when they want, or be too 14.. by sheltering them from the realities of life, it is also true that they should not be too strict. It has also highlighted the disadvantages of the modern 15.. family where the child has only its mother and father to rely on (or the 16.. family, in which the mother or father has to struggle particularly hard to support their 17..). In fact, many believe that we should return to traditional family values and the 18.. family: extensive research has shown that children from these families are generally better behaved and have a better chance of success in later life.

Crime & the law

1 Match the words and phrases in the box with their correct definition 1 – 10.

| barrister | break the law | defendant | judge | jury | law-abiding |
| offender | solicitor | victim | witness |

1. A person appointed to make legal decisions in a court of law. ....

2. A group of 12 citizens who are sworn to decide whether someone is guilty or innocent on the basis of evidence given in a court of law. ....

3. A person who sees something happen or is present when something happens. ....

4. A person who appears in a court of law accused of doing something illegal. ....

5. A person who is attacked or who is in an accident. ....

6. A qualified lawyer who gives advice to members of the public and acts for them in legal matters. ....

7. A person who commits an offence against the law. ....

8. A lawyer who can present a case in court. ....

9. An expression used to describe someone who obeys the law. ....

10. To do something that is illegal. ....

2 The following groups of sentences describe the legal process which follows a crime. However, with the exception of the first sentence, the sentences in each group are in the wrong order. Put them into the correct order, using the key words and phrases in bold to help you. Some of these words appear in Task A.

Part 1

A. One night, Jim Smith **committed** a serious crime. = *Sentence 1*

B. Jim asked the officer for a **solicitor** to help him. ....

C. At the same time, the police arranged for a **barrister** to **prosecute** him. ....

D. They took him to the police station and formally **charged** him with the crime. ....

E. When the **trial** began and he appeared in **court** for the first time, he **pleaded** his **innocence.** ....

F. The next morning the police **arrested** him. ....

Part 2

A. His barrister also said he was **innocent** and asked the court to **acquit** him. = *Sentence 1*

B. While he was in prison, he applied for **parole.** ....

C. As a result, the judge **sentenced** him to two years in prison. ....

D. He was **released** after 18 months. ....

E. However, there were several **witnesses,** and the **evidence** against him was overwhelming. ....

F. Having all the **proof** they needed, the **jury** returned a **guilty verdict.** ....

Part 3

A. Unfortunately, prison failed to **rehabilitate** him and after his **release** he continued with his **misdeeds,** attacking an old woman in the street. = *Sentence 1*

B. Jim promised to **reform** and the pensioner withdrew her call for more severe **retribution.** ....

Crime & the law

C. With this in mind, instead of passing a *custodial sentence,* he *fined* him a lot of money and ordered him to do *community service.* ....

D. He was *re-arrested* and returned to court. ....

E. His new *victim,* a pensioner, thought that the judge was being too *lenient* on Jim and called for the reinstatement of *corporal punishment* and *capital punishment!* ....

F. At his second trial the judge agreed that prison was not a *deterrent* for Jim. ....

3. Now look at this extract from a politician's speech and complete the gaps with one of the words or phrases from Exercises 1 and 2. In some cases, more than one answer may be possible.

Are you worried about crime? I am. We read it every day in the papers. A terrible crime has been 1.. , the police have 2.. someone, he has appeared in front of a jury in a 3.. of law, he has 4.. .... his innocence but has been found 5.. of his crime and he has been 6.. to 10 years in prison. We are all very relieved that the criminal is being punished for his 7.. , and 8.. citizens like you and me can sleep more safely at night.

But what happens next? We all hope, don't we, that the prisoner will benefit from society's 9.. , that a spell in prison will 10.. him and make him a better person. We all hope that he will 11.. and become like us. We all hope that when he is eventually 12.. and let loose on the streets, he will be a good character, the threat of another spell in jail being a suitable 13.. which will stop him from breaking the law again. Oh yes.

But let's face it. The reality is usually very different. The prisoner may be released on 14.. , before the end of his sentence. He will try to re-enter society. But then he often becomes a 15.. himself, unable to find work and rejected by society. It isn't long before he's back in prison again.

So what alternatives are there, I hear you say. What can we do to the 16.. to make sure he doesn't commit another crime? There are alternatives to prison, of course, such as 17.. in which he will provide a service to those around him. Or he can pay a large 18.. . Alternatively, we could establish a more severe system of punishment, including 19.. and 20.. , but we like to consider ourselves civilised, and the idea of beating or executing someone is repellent to us. Oh yes.

The answer, of course, is far simpler. We need to be tough not on the criminal, but on the cause of the crime. We should spend less of the taxpayer's money funding the 21.. and 22.. and all the other people who work for the legal system, and put the money instead into supporting deprived areas which are the breeding grounds for crime. We in the ConLab Party believe that everybody needs a good chance in life, and this is a good step forward. Vote for us now!

Education

1 Look at the sentences below and fill in the gaps using the appropriate word from A, B or C.

1. He didn't get a good grade the first time he did his IELTS exam, so decided to .... it.
   A. resit   *B. remake*   *C. repair*

2. People who attend university later in life are often called .... students.
   A. aged   *B. mature*   *C. old*

3. Although she had left school and was working, she went to evening classes at the local College of .... Education.
   A. Upper   *B. Further*   *C. Higher*

4. After he left school, he decided to go on to .... education and applied for a place at Edinburgh University.
   A. further   *B. upper*   *C. higher*

5. He received a local government .... to help him pay for his course.
   A. fee   *B. fare*   *C. grant*

6. Education helps us to acquire knowledge and learn new ....
   A. skills   *B. powers*   *C. abilities*

7. Although she already had a first degree from university, she decided that she wanted to work towards a .... degree later in life.
   A. further   *B. senior*   *C. higher*

8. We should make the best of every .... to learn.
   A. chance   *B. opportunity*   *C. availability*

9. Nowadays, ... education is promoted a lot in schools.
   A. body   *B. health*   *C. vitality*

10. A large number of parents are dissatisfied with the .... education system, and put their children into private schools instead.
    A. government   *B. national*   *C. state*

11. Because so many students find exams stressful, some colleges offer a system of .... assessment instead.
    A. continual   *B. continuous*   *C. continuing*

12. He has read a lot of books and .... a lot of knowledge.
    A. acquired   *B. won*   *C. achieved*

13. University students have a .... who they meet on a regular basis to discuss their work.
    A. teacher   *B. tutor*   *C. lecturer*

14. There were more than 50 students at Professor Bryant's .... on city planning.
    A. lecture   *B. seminar*   *C. tutorial*

2 Complete the passage on the next page with a suitable word or phrase from the box.

course	day release	degree	discipline	enrol	evening class
graduate	kindergarten	literacy	numeracy	on-line	pass
primary	qualifications	secondary	skills		

Education

When Michael was three years old, he started going to a local (1)..., and two years later began attending his local (2).................................... school, where he learned basic (3).................................... such as (4).................................... and (5).................................... . At the age of 11, he started at (6).................................... school. He wasn't a very keen pupil, and his teachers often complained that he lacked (7).................................... . However, when he took his school-leaving exams, he (8).................................... them all with good grades.

When he left school at the age of 18, he decided he wanted to continue his studies. He found a university which offered a full-time (9).................................... in Modern Art and Design, and (10).................................... on it a few days before his 19th birthday. For three years he worked hard, and (11).................................... with a (12).................................... in Modern Art and Design. After that, he did an (13).................................... course in Photography from a college in the US.

The (14).................................... that he had gained, combined with his creative talents, impressed an advertising agency that he wanted to work for, and they offered him a job. The agency encouraged him to develop his passion for all things creative, and while they weren't prepared to offer him (15).................................... to study during working hours, they paid for him to join an (16).................................... at his local College of Further Education.

3 Now read this essay and complete the gaps with one of the words or phrases from Exercises 1 and 2. You will need to change the form of some of the words.

'You are never too old to learn'. Do you agree with this statement?

Education is a long process that not only provides us with basic (1).................................... such as (2).................................... and (3).................................... , but is also essential in shaping our future lives. From the moment we enter (4).................................... as small children, and as we progress through (5).................................... and (6).................................... education, we are laying the foundations for the life ahead of us. We must (7).................................... ourselves to work hard so that we can (8).................................... exams and gain the (9).................................... we will need to secure a good job. We must also (10).................................... valuable life skills so that we can fit in and work with those around us. And of course (11).................................... education helps us to understand how we can stay fit and healthy.

For most people, this process ends when they are in their mid-to-late teens. For others, however, it is the beginning of a lifetime of learning. After they finish school, many progress to (12).................................... education where they will learn more useful skills such as computer literacy or basic business management. Others will (13).................................... on a programme of (14).................................... education at a university where, with hard work, they will have the opportunity to (15).................................... after three or four years with a well-earned (16).................................... . After that, they may work for a while before opting to study for a (17).................................... degree – an MA, for example, or a PhD. Alternatively, they may choose to attend an (18).................................... after work or, if they have a sympathetic employer, obtain (19).................................... so that they can study during the week. And if they live a long way from a college or university, they might follow an (20).................................... course using the Internet. In fact, it is largely due to the proliferation of computers that many people who have not been near a school for many years, have started to study again and can proudly class themselves as (21).................................... students.

We live in a fascinating and constantly changing world, and we must continually learn and acquire new knowledge if we are to adapt and keep up with changing events. Our schooldays are just the beginning of this process, and we should make the best of every (22) .... to develop ourselves, whether we are 18 or 80. You are, indeed, never too old to learn.

The environment

1 Match the first part of each sentence in the left-hand column with its second part in the right-hand column. Use the words and phrases in bold to help you. Check that each sentence you put together is grammatically correct.

1. Some modern agricultural methods have been heavily criticised,...

2. If you wear a fur coat in public,...

3. It is illegal to kill pandas, tigers...

4. If we don't do more to protect pandas,...

5. A lot of British people are interested in unusual animals,...

6. National parks in Kenya are currently recruiting experts...

7. In an attempt to preserve forests around the country...

8. We would like to carry out more scientific study into rainforests...

9. I don't like zoos because I think...

10. I saw a fascinating documentary about the way animals live in Venezuela and thought...

11. The Chinese government has spent a lot of money...

12. Hunters have killed so many animals that...

(A) ...in many countries *poaching* is considered more serious than drug smuggling.

(B) ...and *rare breeds* parks are very popular with many.

(C) ...in *wildlife management.*

(D) ...the government's *conservation programme* has been very successful.

(E) ...they'll soon be *extinct.*

(F) ...with *battery farming* in particular receiving a lot of condemnation.

(G) ...it was fascinating to observe their *natural behaviour.*

(H) ...on a successful panda *breeding* programme.

(I) ...keeping animals in *captivity* is cruel.

(J) ...or any other *endangered species.*

(K) ...but it is often difficult to get people to fund the *research.*

(L) ...you risk coming under attack from *animal rights activists.*

2 Replace the phrases in bold in these sentences with a word or phrase from the box so that the sentences sound more natural. There are three words or phrases that you do not need.

acid rain	biodegradable packaging	contaminated	deforestation
ecosystem	emissions	environmentalists	erosion	fossil fuels
genetically modified	global warming	green belt	greenhouse
organic	pesticides	pollution	rain forest	recycle things	renewable

1. In Britain, building is restricted or completely banned in the *area of farming land or woods and parks which surrounds a town.* ....

2. Many companies are developing *boxes, cartons and cans which can easily be decomposed by organisms such as bacteria, or by sunlight, sea, water, etc.* ....

3. The burning of some fuels creates *carbon dioxide, carbon monoxide, sulphur dioxide, methane and other* gases which rise into the atmosphere. ....

4. Farmers have cleared hectares of *thick wooded land in tropical regions where the precipitation is very high.* ....

5. Planting trees provides some protection from the *gradual wearing away* of soil. ....

6. We should all try to *process waste material so that it can be used again.* ....

7. These potatoes are *cultivated naturally, without using any chemical fertilisers or pesticides.* ....

8. This bread is made from wheat which has been *altered at a molecular level so as to change certain characteristics which can be inherited.* ....

9. *The process of removing the trees from an area of land* is destroying millions of acres of woodland every year. ....

The environment

10. *Polluted precipitation which kills trees* falls a long distance away from the source of the pollution.
....

11. Human beings have had a devastating effect on the *living things, both large and small,* in many parts of the world. ....

12. The *gases and other substances* which come from factories using oil, coal and other *fuels which are the remains of plants and animals* can cause serious damage to the environment. ....

13. Don't drink that water! It's been *made dirty by something being added to it.* ....

14. Friends of the Earth, Greenpeace and other *people concerned with protecting the environment are holding a forum in London next month.* ....

15. *The heating up of the earth's atmosphere by pollution* is threatening life as we know it.
....

3 Now look at this essay and complete the gaps with one of the words or phrases from Exercises 1 and 2. In some cases, more than one answer will be possible. You may need to change the form of some of the words.

'Environmental degradation is a major world problem. What causes this problem, and what can we do to prevent it?'

There is no doubt that the environment is in trouble. Factories burn 1............................... which produce 2............................... , and this kills trees. At the same time, 3............................... gases rise into the air and contribute to 4............................... , which threatens to melt the polar ice cap. Meanwhile farmers clear huge areas of 5............................... in places such as the Amazon to produce feeding land for cattle or wood for building. Rivers and oceans are so heavily 6............................... by industrial waste that it is no longer safe to go swimming. Cars pump out poisonous 7............................... which we all have to breathe in. 8............................... and overfishing are killing off millions of animals, including whales, elephants and other 9............................... . In fact, all around us, all living things large and small which comprise our finely balanced 10............................... are being systematically destroyed by human greed and thoughtlessness.

There is a lot we can all do, however, to help prevent this. The easiest thing, of course, is to 11............................... waste material such as paper and glass so that we can use it again. We should also check that the things we buy from supermarkets are packaged in 12............................... packaging which decomposes easily. At the same time, we should make a conscious effort to avoid foods which are 13............................... (at least until someone proves that they are safe both for us and for the environment). If you are truly committed to protecting the environment, of course, you should only buy 14............................... fruit and vegetables, safe in the knowledge that they have been naturally cultivated. Finally, of course, we should buy a smaller car, as these cause less 15............................... than large saloons or SUVs. Even better, we should try to make more use of public transport.

The serious 16............................... , however, do much more. They are aware of the global issues involved and will actively involve themselves in 17............................... by making sure our forests are kept safe for future generations. They will oppose activities which are harmful to animals, such as 18............................... . And they will campaign to keep the 19............................... around our towns and cities free from new building.

We cannot all be as committed as them, but we can at least do our own little bit at grass roots level. We, as humans, have inherited the earth, but that doesn't mean we can do whatever we like with it.

Food & diet

1 Look at the dictionary definitions, and arrange the letters in bold to form the words they are defining. The first letter of each word is <u>underlined</u>. Write your answers in the crossword on the next page. (Each definition is followed by a sample sentence in *italics* with the word removed).

1. Natural substances found in food that are necessary to keep your body healthy. Each one is given a name using a letter of the alphabet. **ai<u>m</u>vistn** (*Apples contain several essential _____*)

2. Of food: providing the substances that people need in order to be healthy. **<u>n</u>itsortiuu** (*A healthy, _____ meal*)

3. Someone who chooses not to eat meat or fish. **geet<u>r</u>vanai** (*I've been a _____ since I was 13*)

4. Substances found in food that supply your body with heat and energy. **bo<u>c</u>aratydesrh** (*Bread, potatoes and rice are a good source of _____*)

5. A substance found in food such as meat, eggs and milk that people need in order to grow and be strong. **<u>p</u>ntiroe** (*Children who lack sufficient _____ in their diet are often ill*)

6. A substance in your blood that can cause heart disease if you have too much of it. **ero<u>c</u>lshtloe.** (*There are many foods that claim to reduce _____ levels*)

7. A serious lack of food that continues for a long time and causes many people in a country to become ill or die. **an<u>f</u>eim** (*The crop failure caused widespread _____ in the region*)

8. A condition in which someone is too fat, in a way that is dangerous for their health. **e<u>o</u>itbys** (*The report highlighted the problems caused by childhood _____*)

9. Weak or ill because you do not eat enough, or because you do not eat enough of the right foods. **l<u>n</u>omaisheurd** (*24 per cent of children in the school were found to be _____*)

10. Natural substances found in some foods that you need for good health. **a<u>m</u>erlins** (*Milk contains calcium, one of the most important _____ for maintaining strong bones*)

11. Oil found in meat. **ta<u>f</u>.** (*You should trim the _____ off meat before you cook it*)

12. The parts of fruit, vegetables and grain that your body cannot digest. **br<u>f</u>ie** (*Dietary _____ helps protect us from disease*)

13. Heavier than you should be. **w<u>o</u>rigvehet** (*I'm a couple of kilogrammes _____*)

14. Food that has recently been picked, caught or prepared. **s<u>f</u>rhe** (*_____ vegetables are much nicer than frozen ones*)

15. Units for measuring how much energy you get from food. **ri<u>c</u>lesao** (*There are over 150 _____ in a small packet of crisps*)

16. Describing food that has had chemicals or other substances added to it. **<u>p</u>ercedsos** (*_____ meat keeps for longer than natural meat*)

Food & diet

2 Match sentences 1 – 10 with a second sentence A – J. Use the key words and phrases in bold to help you. In some cases, more than one answer is possible.

1. A lot of people are **allergic** to nuts

2. Many people do not trust **genetically modified** foods.

3. **Organic** fruit and vegetables are quite expensive, but may be better for you.

4. I refuse to eat eggs from **battery chickens**.

5. I only eat meat from **free range** animals.

6. The **harvest** has been very bad this year.

7. If the drought continues, there will be serious food **shortages**.

8. There has been an increase in cases of **salmonella**, **listeria**, **e.coli** and other types of **food poisoning**.

9. Too many people fail to eat a **balanced diet**.

10. **Fast food** is very popular.

A. This is because they are cultivated naturally, without using any chemical fertilisers or pesticides.

B. As a result, we may have to import a lot of basic foods.

C. They are not sure that altering the composition of cells to change certain characteristics is safe.

D. I like to know that the animals have enough space to express their natural behaviour.

E. Too much rain has prevented crops from ripening properly.

F. This is in spite of the fact that it is fattening and unhealthy.

G. It can be difficult to trace the sources of some of these.

H. They should make an effort to consume sufficient quantities of the different food groups.

I. They have a bad physical reaction if they eat them.

J. Animals should not spend their lives confined in small cages.

Food & diet

3 Complete this article with the words and phrases from Exercises 1 and 2. In some cases, more than one answer is possible.

Children love eating (1)......................................, but burgers, chicken nuggets and other heavily (2)...................................... food products not only contain a large number of unhealthy chemicals and other additives, but also lack the essential (3)...................................... and (4)...................................... that a child needs. In addition, they also contain a lot of (5)...................................... and (6)...................................... which, if eaten in quantity, can result in childhood (7)...................................... (in fact, a recent survey suggests that 39 per cent of 8 – 15 year-olds are seriously overweight).

Many children end up (8)......................................, since they eat too much of the wrong sort of food. In fact, in many parts of the developed world, a lot of children show similar symptoms to those in poorer developing countries, where food (9)...................................... cause thousands of deaths from starvation, especially in the wake of natural disasters which ruin crops and in some cases totally destroy the annual (10)...................................... . Furthermore, the large amounts of (11)...................................... in animal and dairy products (a common feature of fast food) are believed to be partly responsible for increased cases of heart disease in young people, a recent phenomenon that is causing great concern.

It is therefore important children learn the benefits of eating a (12)......................................, as it is important they consume sufficient quantities of the different food groups. They should be encouraged to eat more (13)...................................... fruit and vegetables, and also more food that is high in (14)...................................... They should still be allowed the occasional burger or pizza, but these should be seen as an occasional treat rather than forming the main part of their diet.

Geography

1 Put the words and phrases in each list in the first box in order according to their sizes. (1 = the smallest, 4 = the largest). In each list, there is one word that does not belong with the others.

1. forest • tree • copse • beach • wood
2. road • peak • footpath • track • lane
3   mountain • hillock • shore • hill • mountain range
4. gorge • plain • waterfall • hollow • valley
5. gulf • ridge • inlet • bay • cove
6. cliff • brook • river • estuary • stream
7. city • continent • tributary • county • country
8. pond • ocean • sea • cape • lake

1. 1 ....,	2 ....,	3 ....,	4 ....
2. 1 ....,	2 ....,	3 ....,	4 ....
3. 1 ....,	2 ....,	3 ....,	4 ....
4. 1 ....,	2 ....,	3 ....,	4 ....
5. 1 ....,	2 ....,	3 ....,	4 ....
6. 1 ....,	2 ....,	3 ....,	4 ....
7. 1 ....,	2 ....,	3 ....,	4 ....
8. 1 ....,	2 ....,	3 ....,	4 ....

2 Put these words and phrases into their correct category in the boxes below and on the next page. Some can be included in more than one category.

beach   cape   cliff   coast   coastline   conurbation   depopulation
densely populated   fertile   glacier   highlands   industrialised
irrigation   mountainous   mouth   overcrowding   peak   peninsula
plateau   ridge   shore   source   summit   tributary   under-developed
urban sprawl   vegetation   waterfall

Geographical features associated with water and the sea

Geographical features associated with land, hills and mountains

Geography

Words and phrases associated with agriculture and rural land	Words and phrases associated with towns and cities

---

3 Complete this report of a journey with words and phrases from Exercises 1 and 2. In some cases, more than one answer is possible.

We began our journey in the capital, Trinifuegos, a 1.. conurbation of almost 10 million. It is not a pretty place; heavily 2.. , with huge factories belching out black fumes, and miles of 3.. as housing estates and shopping centres spread out from the 4.. centre for miles. It was a relief to leave.

As soon as we got into the countryside, things improved considerably. The climate is dry and it is difficult to grow anything, but thanks to 5.. , which helps bring water in from the Rio Cauto (the huge river with its 6.. high up in the snow-covered 7.. of the Sierra Maestra 8..), the land is fertile enough to grow the sugar cane on which much of the economy is based. We saw few people, however, as many have moved to the towns and cities to look for more profitable work. It is largely due to this rural 9.. that the sugar-cane industry is suffering.

Further south and we entered the Holguin 10.. , with mountains rising high above us on both sides. The land here drops sharply to the sea and the slow-moving waters of the Rio Cauto give way to 11.. which tumble over cliffs, and small, fast-moving 12.. which are not even wide enough to take a boat. At this point, the road we were travelling along became a 13.. which was only just wide enough for our vehicle, and then an unpaved 14.. which almost shook the vehicle to pieces.

And then suddenly, the Pacific 15.. was in front of us. Our destination was the town of Santiago de Gibara, built on a 16.. sticking out into the blue waters. The countryside here undulates gently, with low 17.. covered in rich tropical jungle. The open 18.. surrounding the 19.. of the Rio Cauto as it reaches the ocean is rich and 20.. , ideal for growing the tobacco plants which need a lot of warm, damp soil.

That night I lay in my cheap hotel, listening to the waves gently lapping the 21.. , and when I eventually fell asleep, I dreamt of the people who had first inhabited this 22.. almost 2,000 years before.

Global problems

1 Complete sentences 1 – 15 with the correct word or phrase from A, B or C. In each case two of the options are incorrectly spelt.

1. Thousands of buildings were flattened in the San Francisco .... of 1906.
   A. earthquack   B. earthquake   C. earthquaik

2. The .... damaged properties all along the coast.
   A. hurricane   B. hurriccane   C. huriccane

3. A .... struck the southern coast with tremendous force.
   A. tornadoe   B. tornado   C. tornaddo

4. The .... caused immense damage in the regions along the coast.
   A. taifun   B. typhone   C. typhoon

5. The .... has been dormant for years, but last month it showed signs of new life.
   A. volcano   B. vulcano   C. volcanoe

6. Several .... were heard during the night as the army occupied the city.
   A. explossions   B. explosiones   C. explosions

7. The American .... of 1861–1865 was fought between the south and the north.
   A. civil war   B. sivil war   C. civvil war

8. There has been a major .... on the motorway.
   A. acident   B. accident   C. acciddent

9. .... rain has brought serious problems.
   A. Torrential   B. Torential   C. Torrantial

10. The storm caused widespread .... along the coast.
    A. devvastation   B. devustation   C. devastation

11. The .... were caused by heavy rain.
    A. floodes   B. floods   C. flouds

12. Relief workers are bringing food to ....-stricken areas.
    A. draught   B. drought   C. drouhgt

13. .... is widespread in parts of Africa, with millions suffering from malnutrition.
    A. Famine   B. Fammine   C. Faminne

14. The authorities are taking steps to prevent an .... of cholera.
    A. epidemmic   B. epidemic   C. eppidemic

15. The .... was spread from rats to fleas and then on to humans.
    A. plague   B. plaque   C. plaigue

2 Complete the sentences with an appropriate word or phrase from the box. In some cases, more than one answer is possible.

broke out   casualties   disaster   erupted   refugees   relief   shook
spread   suffering   survivors

1. The disease .... rapidly, killing everybody in its path.
2. The fire .... through the slums, destroying everything.

3. When the volcano .... , people panicked and tried to escape.

4. The ground .... violently when the earthquake began.

5. Fierce fighting .... between government soldiers and rebel forces.

6. A funeral was held for the .... of the fire.

7. An aid convoy was sent to help .... of the hurricane.

8. .... from the conflict in Mantagua have been fleeing across the border.

9. The poor people in the city have experienced terrible .... as a result of the disaster.

10. International aid agencies are trying to bring .... to the starving population.

3 Complete this report with words and phrases from Exercises 1 and 2. In some cases, more than one answer is possible.

REPORT FROM THE INTERNATIONAL CHARITIES SUPPORT FOUNDATION (ICSF)

The last year has been a particularly busy one for the ICSF. Outlined below are a few of the areas we have been busy in.

1. Following 1... rain in eastern Mozamlumbi in January, millions were made homeless as 2... waters rose. The water also became polluted and there was a cholera 3... as people continued to use it for drinking and cooking. Furthermore, as the harvest had been destroyed and there was not enough food to go round, 4... became a problem. Charities around the world worked particularly hard to bring 5... to the area.

2. Mount Etsuvius, the 6... which had been dormant since 1968, 7... suddenly in April. Thousands had to be evacuated to camps 30 miles from the disaster area. They still have not been rehoused.

3. The 8... in the Caribbean in July, which saw wind speeds of up to 180 miles per hour, caused immense 9... on many islands. Islands off the Japanese coast also suffered their worst 10... in almost 30 years, with prolonged winds in excess of 150 miles per hour. There were many 11... who had to be evacuated to hospitals which were not properly equipped to deal with the disasters.

4. The 12... in the northern part of Somopia continued into its second year, with millions of acres of crops destroyed by lack of rain. Meanwhile, the 13... between those loyal to the president and those supporting the rebel leader continued into its fifth year. 14... from the conflict have been fleeing across the border, with stories of atrocities committed by both sides.

5. In October, a fire 15... through Londum, the ancient capital of Perania. The 16..., which probably started in a bakery, destroyed thousands of homes. There were several 17... when the fire reached a fireworks factory, and a number of people were killed.

6. An outbreak of bubonic 18... was reported in the eastern provinces of Indocuba in November. It is believed to have been caused by a sudden increase in the number of rats breeding in the sewers.

A full report will be available in February, and will be presented to the appropriate departments of the United Nations shortly afterwards.

Healthcare

1 Match the sentence in the left-hand column with a sentence in the right-hand column. Use the words and phrases in bold to help you.

PROBLEMS

1. Mrs Brady has suffered from terrible *rheumatism* for years.

2. More women than men are affected by *arthritis.*

3. Air conditioning units are often responsible for spreading *infections* around an office.

4. *Cardiovascular disease* is becoming more common in Britain.

5. Too much exposure to the sun can cause skin *cancer.*

6. It is important not to eat too much food with a high *cholesterol* content.

7. Too many people these days live a *sedentary lifestyle.*

8. People in positions of responsibility often have *stress-related* illnesses.

9. Premature babies are *vulnerable* to illnesses.

10. Healthcare professionals say that hospitals around the country are suffering from serious *underfunding*.

11. The AIDS *virus* is *incurable.*

12. The country is currently experiencing its worst *flu epidemic* for over 30 years.

(A) Illnesses which affect the *circulation* of blood are particularly common with people who are overweight.

(B) This is deposited on the walls of the *arteries* and can block them.

(C) They can easily be spread from one person to another.

(D) Pains or stiffness in the *joints* or *muscles* can be very difficult to live with.

(E) They don't get enough exercise.

(F) This is because their *immune system* is not properly developed.

(G) Anyone who has caught the *virus* is reminded that it cannot be treated with *antibiotics*, and they should stay inside until the *symptoms* have passed.

(H) The painful *inflammation* of a joint may require *surgery.*

(I) However, the government denies it has made *cutbacks* to the National Health Service.

(J) However there are drugs which can slow down its cell-destroying properties.

(K) Once the body's *cells* start growing abnormally, a cure can be difficult to find.

(L) The pressures of a high-powered job can cause nervous *strain,* which may require drugs.

---

2 Replace the words or phrases in bold in these sentences with a word or phrase from the box so that the sentence sounds more natural. There are three words or phrases that you do not need.

CURES

active   a diet   consultant   conventional medicine   debilitating
diagnose   holistic medicine   minerals   operation   protein   surgeon
therapeutic   traditional medicines   vitamins   welfare state

1. If you suffer from a bad back, a massage may be *able to cure or relieve the disorder*.

2. One of the secrets of remaining in good health is to choose *food to eat* that is high in fibre and low in fat.

3. Most people, when they are ill, rely on *modern pills and tablets* to cure them.

4. Some *old-fashioned cures for illnesses,* such as herbal tablets and remedies, are becoming increasingly popular.

5. Many people are turning to *treatments which involve the whole person, including their mental health, rather than just dealing with the symptoms of the illness.*

6. Doctors sometimes refer their patients to a *medical specialist attached to a hospital.*

7. It takes many years of training to become a *doctor specialising in surgery.*

8. Meat, eggs and nuts are rich sources of *a compound which is an essential part of living cells, and which is essential to keep the human body working properly.*

9. On his holiday, he had to take *essential substances which are not synthesised by the body but are found in food and are needed for growth and health,* because the food he ate lacked the B and C groups.

10. Calcium and zinc are two of the most important *substances found in food.*

11. Most doctors recommend an *energetic* lifestyle, with plenty of exercise.

12. British people enjoy free healthcare thanks to the *large amount of money which is spent to make sure they have adequate health services.*

3 Now look at this extract from a magazine article and complete the gaps with one of the words or phrases from Exercises 1 and 2. In some cases, more than one answer may be possible.

A cure for the future in the past?

For over 50 years, the people of Britain have relied on the 1........................ to make sure they have adequate health services. But now the National Health Service is sick. Government 2........................ and 3........................ are forcing hospitals to close, and waiting lists for treatment are getting longer. Under such circumstances, it is no surprise that more people are turning to private (but expensive) healthcare.

For some, however, there are alternatives. They are turning their backs on modern pills, tablets and other 4........................ . It seems paradoxical, but in an age of microchips and high technology, 5........................ (the old-fashioned cures that our grandparents relied on) is making a comeback. Consider these case studies:

Maude is 76 and has been suffering from 6........................ for almost 10 years. "The inflammation in my joints was almost unbearable, and my doctor referred me to a 7........................ at the London Hospital. I was told that I needed 8........................ , but would need to wait for at least two years before I could have the operation. In desperation, I started having massage sessions. To my surprise, these were very 9........................ , and while they didn't cure the disorder, they did relieve it to some extent."

Ron is 46. His high-powered city job was responsible for a series of 10........................ illnesses, and the drugs he took did little to relieve the nervous strain. "I read about treatments which involve the whole person rather than the individual 11........................ , but I had always been sceptical about 12........................ . However, my friend recommended a dietician who advised me that part of my problem was 13........................-related. Basically, the foods I was eating were contributing to my disorder. She gave me a list of foods that would provide the right 14........................ and 15........................ to keep me in good health. At the same time, she recommended a more 16........................ lifestyle – running, swimming, that kind of thing. I'm a bit of a couch potato, and the 17........................ lifestyle I had lived was compounding the problem. Now I feel great!"

So is there still a place in our lives for modern medicine? While it is true that some infections and viruses may be prevented by resorting to alternative medicine, more serious illnesses such as 18........................ need more drastic measures. We do need our health service at these times, and we shouldn't stop investing in its future. But we mustn't forget that for some common illnesses, the cure may lie in the past.

The media

1 Match the words and phrases in the box with their definitions 1 – 12. Write the word or phrase after each definition.

> broadcasts   broadsheets   coverage   current affairs   download
> information overload   the Internet   journalists   log on   reporters
> tabloids   website

1. Large-format quality newspapers ....

2. Small-format newspapers ....

3. People who write for newspapers or periodicals ....

4. The amount of space or time given to an event in newspapers or on television ....

5. Political, social and economic events that are happening now ....

6. Radio or television programmes ....

7. To enter a password and start to access a computer system ....

8. People who write articles or make broadcasts about events in the news ....

9. To transfer pages from a website on to your own computer ....

10. The international network linking millions of computers ....

11. An expression referring to the inability of a human to process everything he or she sees or hears ....

12. A collection of on-line pages created by a company, organisation or individual ....

2 Complete this extract from a television interview with an appropriate word or phrase from the box.

> censorship   chequebook journalism   entertainment   exploiting
> freedom of the press   gutter press   information   integrity
> invasion of privacy   investigative journalism   libel   media tycoon
> paparazzi   readership   unscrupulous

Interviewer: Welcome to today's programme. Today we will be discussing the 1..., and asking the question: Should we allow newspapers and television channels to print or say whatever they like? In the studio I have television personality Timothy Blake and 2.. Rupert Poubelle, multi-millionaire owner of the *Daily Views* newspaper. Timothy, let's start with you.

T.B.: Thank you. In my opinion, it's time the government imposed stricter 3.. of the press in order to prevent 4.. journalists and reporters from making money by 5.. people. I have often accused Mr Poubelle's organisation of 6.. – nowadays I can't even sunbathe in my garden without being photographed by his hordes of 7.. . They're like vultures. And everything they print about me is lies, complete rubbish.

Interviewer: But isn't it true that the media provides us with valuable 8.. and 9.. , and censorship would deprive us of much of this? Rupert?

R.P.: Of course, Mr, Blake's accusations are unfounded, as are the accusations of 10.................................... we have received. However, I can safely say that the *Daily Views* never pays people huge amounts of money for stories. We have far too much 11.................................... for that. And don't forget that my paper also has an excellent reputation for 12.................................... . Remember it was us who uncovered corruption in the banking system, and ran a series of articles on child labour in clothing factories. We give our 13.................................... what they want, and that's what really counts.

T.B.: But most of what you report isn't really news. And a lot of it is just a big pile of lies. Sensational stories made up to entertain people. Typical 14.................................... behaviour, in other words. I'm amazed nobody has sued you for 15.................................... yet.

---

3 Now read this essay and complete the gaps with one of the words or phrases from Exercises 1 and 2. You will need to change the form of some of the words.

'The media plays a valuable role in keeping us informed and entertained. However, many people believe it has too much power and freedom.' Discuss your views on this, giving examples and presenting a balanced argument both in favour of, and against, the power and freedom of the media.

Barely a hundred years ago, if we wanted to stay informed about what was going on in the world, we had to rely on word of mouth or, at best, newspapers. But because communication technology was very basic, the news we received was often days or weeks old.

We still have newspapers, of course, but they have changed almost beyond recognition. Whether we choose to read the 1.................................... , with their quality 2.................................... of news and other 3.................................... by top 4.................................... and articles by acclaimed 5.................................... , or we prefer the popular 6.................................... , with their lively gossip and colourful stories, we are exposed to a wealth of information barely conceivable at the beginning of the last century.

We also have television and radio. News 7.................................... let us know about world events practically as they happen, while sitcoms, chat shows and documentaries, etc. keep us entertained and informed. And there is also 8.................................... , where we can access information from millions of 9.................................... around the world which we can then 10.................................... on to our own computers.

However, these forms of 11.................................... and 12.................................... (or 'infotainment' as they are sometimes collectively called) have their negative side. Famous personalities frequently accuse the 13.................................... (and sometimes even respectable papers) of 14.................................... by gangs of 15.................................... who follow them around with their cameras and long lenses. Newspapers are often accused of 16.................................... by angry politicians who hate reading damaging lies about themselves, and there are frequent accusations of 17...................................., with 18.................................... reporters paying people vast sums of money to tell them about the crime they committed or what their famous neighbour has been up to. Of course, it's not just the papers which are to blame. Television companies have cast their 19.................................... aside to get a good story, and you cannot even 20.................................... to the Internet without seeing something shocking or unacceptable. 21.................................... argue that they are just giving people what they want, but in my opinion, people should not always *get* what they want.

Many argue that the government should impose stricter 22.................................... to prevent such things happening. But others argue that 23.................................... is the keystone of a free country. Personally, I take the view that while the media may occasionally abuse its position of power, the benefits greatly outweigh the disadvantages. Our lives would be much emptier without the wealth of information available to us today, and we are better people as a result.

Men & women

1 Look at the words and phrases in bold in these sentences and decide if we generally consider them to have a <u>positive</u> connotation or a <u>negative</u> connotation.

1   They would never admit it, but men and women are in a continuous **power struggle** at work. *Positive / Negative*

2   Most major companies are **male-dominated**.   *Positive / Negative*

3   It's a fact that, when it comes to promoting their employees, some companies still **discriminate** on the basis of someone's sex.   *Positive / Negative*

4   A recent survey suggests that many professional women working for large companies and organisations often hit a **glass ceiling** at some point in their career.   *Positive / Negative*

5   Professional businesswomen, especially those in senior management positions, are more **astute** than men.   *Positive / Negative*

6   In my experience, they are also more **versatile**.   *Positive / Negative*

7   What's more, they are better at **multi-tasking**.   *Positive / Negative*

8   They can also be much more **ruthless** when necessary.   *Positive / Negative*

9   My elder brother is such a **male chauvinist**!   *Positive / Negative*

10 As far he is concerned, women are little more than **sex objects**.   *Positive / Negative*

11 He is completely **unreconstructed**.   *Positive / Negative*

12 Some might say that he's a bit of a **dinosaur**.   *Positive / Negative*

13 My younger brother, on the other hand, has **egalitarian** views.   *Positive / Negative*

14 He believes in **equality** between men and women.   *Positive / Negative*

15 He doesn't think that women are the **weaker sex**.   *Positive / Negative*

2 Use the words and phrases in the box to complete the conversation.

battle of the sexes   breadwinner   child rearing   gender roles   household management   male counterparts   practical   role division   Sex Discrimination Act   social convention   stereotypes

Chris: I think that cleaning and cooking are a woman's job. After all, men are no good at
          1... .

Sam: I disagree.

Chris: And in the workplace, women aren't very 2................................, are they?.

Sam: In what way?

Men & women

Chris: In the way that there are a lot of things they can't do as well as men can. Such as, er, well, I can't think of anything in particular at the moment.

Sam: Exactly.

Chris: Well, let's face it, women never do as well as their 3..................................... at work.

Sam: I've never heard such unreconstructed rubbish. Thank goodness the 4.....................................
exists to prevent your views being put into practice. And I suppose you think that women are only good for changing babies' nappies, and other tedious aspects of 5..................................... .

Chris: No, but I do believe that in a modern household, there should be a clearly defined 6..................................... . Men are good at DIY, for example. Most women aren't. And I'll always believe that it's the man who should be the 7....................................., providing food and shelter for his family.

Sam: Well, all I can say is that I'm glad your ideas of 8..................................... are not shared by most people.

Chris: Nonsense! A lot of people believe in traditional 9.....................................: the man goes out to work, the woman stays at home. It's as simple as that.

Sam: Men at work and women at home? Come on, love, those are such typical 10..................................... . With people like you around, the 11..................................... will continue to rage on and on.

Chris: Oh give it a rest, Dad. I'm right, and you know I am.

Sam: Sorry, Christine, but we're in the twenty-first century now. You need to move with the times.

3 Complete this essay with words and phrases from Exercises 1 and 2. In some cases, more than one answer is possible.

A totally 1..................................... society, in which sexual 2.....................................
between men and women is the norm, is still a long way off. This is certainly the case if you watch certain television programmes, where men are often portrayed as the 3.....................................,
bringing money home to the wife, who is often depicted as the 4....................................., prone to extreme emotions and temper tantrums. But is this really the case? Is it still fair to create 5..................................... such as this? After all, as more women go out to work, and more men stay at home to look after the house and children, it is becoming clear that so-called 6..................................... are merging and disappearing.

Men & women

Take the office workplace as an example. For years, businesses and companies were 7.................................. The directors, managers and other senior executives were always male, the secretaries and personal assistants almost always female. This was probably because men were traditionally seen as more 8....................................., more able to deal with the cut-and-thrust of business. However, now women are proving that they can be just as tough, if not tougher, while simultaneously being more 9.................................... and caring. In fact, in many ways, women are much better at 10....................................., which is vital in modern business where you are expected to do more than one job. And thanks to the 11..................................., women are paid the same as men. It would appear that, in many cases, the 12..................................... is a dying breed (although, unfortunately, there are still many 13.................................... men in the workplace who think they can do everything and anything better than their female colleagues, and there are still cases where women climbing up through the ranks get to a point where they hit a 14.................................... and cannot climb any higher).

At home, too, there is less evidence of 15.................................... . It is no longer the woman who does all the cooking, cleaning and 16.................................... . Such 17.................................... is now often shared equally. 18.................................... no longer expects the woman to stay indoors all day while the man stays out until all hours.

The good news, therefore, is that women no longer need to feel they are regarded as mere 19...................................., or the underdogs in a 20.................................... with their 21.................................... . In fact, many believe that in the 22....................................., it is women who have come out on top.

Money & finance

1 Use a dictionary to find the differences between the words and phrases in bold in the following groups.

1. make *a profit* & make *a loss*
2. *extravagant* & *frugal / economical*
3. a *current account* & a *deposit account*
4. a *loan* & a *mortgage*
5. to *deposit* money & to *withdraw money*
6. a *wage* & a *salary*
7. *broke* & *bankrupt*
8. *shares, stocks,* & *dividends*
9. *income tax* & *excise duty*
10. to *credit* & to *debit*
11. a *bank* & a *building society*
12. a *discount* & a *refund*
13. something which was a *bargain*, something which was *overpriced* and something which was *exorbitant*
14. *worthless* & *priceless*
15. *save money* & *invest money*
16. *inflation* & *deflation*
17. *income* & *expenditure*
18. to *lend* & to *borrow*

2 Match the sentences in column A with the sentences in column B. Use the words and phrases in bold to help you.

Column A	Column B
1. The managing director believes the company should start producing pocket computers.	A. I'm really looking forward to spending my *pension.*
2. I always put my money in a building society and not in a bank.	B. The *cost of living* seems to go up every day.
3. I can't afford to buy a new car right now. I don't have enough money.	C. Of course, it's always so difficult to *economise.*
4. I always spend a lot of money when I go on holiday.	D. Shops all over the country are making huge *reductions* on just about everything.
5. I came into a lot of money recently when my uncle died.	E. Then I get home to find out I've **run up** a huge **overdraft** at the bank.
6. Look at this cheque that came in the post this morning from Revenue and Customs.	F. Of course, the potential global *market* for them is enormous.
7. I've been spending too much recently.	G. Fortunately I receive *unemployment benefit.*
8. In my country, there are a lot of very poor people and only a few rich ones.	H. There is a very uneven *distribution of wealth.*
9. I lost my job last month.	I. The *interest* they pay me is much higher.
10. I retire next month.	J. It's the first time I've *inherited* something.
11. Prices are rising quickly everywhere.	K. It seems to be some kind of tax *rebate.*
12. The January sales start tomorrow.	L. Maybe I should consider getting one *on credit.*

3 Now read this passage and complete the gaps with one of the words or phrases from Exercises 1 and 2. You may need to change the form of some of the words.

Financial advice from a father to a son.

In the play *Hamlet* by William Shakespeare, a father gives his son some financial advice. 'Neither a borrower nor a lender be', he says. He is trying to tell his son that he should never 1.. money from anyone because it will make it difficult for him to manage his finances. Likewise he should never give a financial 2.. to a friend because he will probably never see the money again, and will probably lose his friend as well.

Money & finance

The play was written over 400 years ago, but today many parents would give similar advice to their children. Imagine the conversation they would have now:

Son: Right, Dad, I'm off to university now.

Father: All right, son, but let me give you some sound financial advice before you go.

Son: Oh come on, Dad.....

Father: Now listen, this is important. The first thing you should do is to make sure you balance your 3.................................... – the money you receive from me – and your 4.................................... – the money you spend. If you spend too much, you will end up with an 5.................................... at the bank. Don't expect me to pay it for you.

Son: But it's so difficult. Things are so expensive, and the 6.................................... goes up all the time. 7.................................... is running at about 10 per cent.

Father: I know, but you should try to 8.................................... . Avoid expensive shops and restaurants. Also, put your money in a good 9.................................... . They offer a much higher rate of 10.................................... than banks. Also, avoid buying things 11.................................... .

Son: Why?

Father: Because shops charge you an 12.................................... amount of money to buy things over a period of time. It's much better to 13.................................... a little bit of money each week so that when you see something you want, you can buy it outright. Try to wait for the sales, when shops offer huge 14.................................... and you can pick up a 15.................................... . And try to get a 16.................................... .

Son: How do I do that?

Father: Easy. When you buy something, ask the shop if they'll lower the price by, say, 10 per cent. Next, when you eventually get a job and are earning a good salary, try to 17.................................... the money in a good company. Buy 18.................................... in government organisations or 19.................................... in private companies.

Son: OK, Dad, I've heard enough.

Father: One final piece of advice, son.

Son: What's that, Dad?

Father: To thine own self be true.

Son: You what?

1 Choose the most suitable explanation or interpretation, A or B, for the following sentences. Use the words and phrases in bold to help you.

1. People enjoy the *mobility* that owning a car gives them.
   A. People enjoy being able to travel easily from one place to another.
   B. People enjoy being able to drive very fast.

2. What's your *destination*?
   A. Where have you come from?
   B. Where are you going to?

3. *Congestion* in the city centre has increased dramatically.
   A. It is now easier to drive around the city centre than it was before.
   B. It is now more difficult to drive around the city centre than it was before.

4. The local council wants to reduce the risks to *pedestrians.*
   A. The local council wants to make it safer for people to walk along the street.
   B. The local council wants to make it safer for drivers and their passengers.

5. The *pollution* in my city is terrible.
   A. The air quality in my city is very poor.
   B. There is a lot of crime in my city.

6. *Traffic-calming* measures are becoming increasingly common throughout the country.
   A. People have to drive more slowly because of the increased number of police in villages and towns.
   B. People have to drive more carefully through towns and villages because of specially-built obstacles in the road.

7. The centre of Camford has been designated a *traffic-free zone.*
   A. You cannot take your car into the centre of Camford.
   B. You can park your car for free in the centre of Camford.

8. Container lorries and other large vehicles *dominate* our roads.
   A. There are a lot of large vehicles on the roads.
   B. There aren't many large vehicles on the roads.

9. Young drivers have a higher *accident risk* than older drivers.
   A. Young drivers are more likely than older drivers to be involved in a crash.
   B. Young drivers are less likely than older drivers to be involved in a crash.

10. Public transport is heavily *subsidised* in most areas.
    A. The government has made public transport cheaper to use by giving money to bus and train companies.
    B. The government has made public transport more expensive to use by increasing the price of road tax.

11. The junction of London Road and Holly Street is an accident *black spot.*
    A. A lot of traffic accidents happen here.
    B. Not many accidents happen here.

12. The city council needs to adopt an effective *transport strategy* within the next five years.
    A. The city council needs to find a better way for people to get into, around and out of the city.
    B. The city council needs to encourage more drivers to bring their cars into the city.

On the road

2 Look at sentences 1 – 10 and decide what has, or hasn't, happened (sentences A – J). Use the words and phrases in bold to help you.

1. Ambulance driver to policeman: 'The **pedestrian's injuries** are very severe and he has to go to hospital.'
2. Judge to driver: '**Drink-driving** is a serious offence and I therefore ban you from driving for a year.'
3. Driving instructor to student driver: 'Stop! That's a **pedestrian crossing**!'
4. Examiner to student driver: 'You don't know enough about **the Highway Code** yet to pass your theory test.'
5. Policeman to driver: 'Do you realise you were **speeding** back there, sir?'
6. Driver to a friend: 'I can't believe it! He gave me a heavy **fine** and six points on my licence.'
7. Police officer to radio interviewer: '**Joyriding** has increased by almost 50 per cent and I am urging everyone to think twice before they get involved in this stupid activity.'
8. Television news presenter: 'So far this year there have been 27 **fatalities** on Oxfordshire's roads.'
9. City council officer to journalist: 'As part of our new transport strategy, we are going to construct **cycle lanes** in and around the city.'
10. City council officer to journalist: 'The **"Park and Ride"** scheme has been very successful over the last year.'

A. Somebody is unfamiliar with the government publication containing the rules for people travelling on roads.
B. More people have been leaving their cars in designated areas outside a city and catching a bus into the city centre.
C. A lot of cars have been stolen, mainly by young people who want some excitement.
D. A person walking in the street has been hit and badly hurt by a vehicle.
E. Somebody has decided to make it safer to use bicycles.
F. Somebody has almost driven through a red light and hit a person walking across the road.
G. Somebody has had to pay money because of a driving offence.
H. Somebody has consumed an illegal amount of alcohol before driving their car.
I. A lot of people have been killed in traffic-related accidents.
J. Somebody has been driving too fast.

3. Complete this article with the words and phrases in Exercises 1 and 2. In some cases, more than one answer is possible, and you will need to change some of the word forms.

1.................................. and 2.................................. on Britain's roads are increasing from year to year: last year, 2,827 people were killed and almost 300,000 hurt in traffic-related accidents. Most of these were caused by drivers 3.................................. in built-up areas, where many seem to disregard the 30mph limit, or 4.................................. , especially around Christmas, when more alcohol is consumed than at any other time. In many cases, it is 5.................................. who are the victims, knocked down as they are walking across the street at 6.................................. by drivers who seem to have forgotten that the rules of the 7.................................. order you to stop at red lights.

But these innocent victims, together with the help of the police and local councils, are fighting back. In Oxford, a city plagued by 8.................................. and 9.................................. caused by traffic, and a notorious accident 10.................................. for pedestrians and cyclists, the city council has recently implemented its new 11.................................. , which has improved the flow of traffic to the benefit of those on foot or on two wheels. 12.................................. measures such as bollards and speed humps have slowed traffic down. 13.................................. schemes have helped reduce the number of cars in the city, as office workers and shoppers leave their cars outside the city and bus in instead. Cornmarket Street, the main shopping thoroughfare, has been designated a 14.................................. , closed to all vehicles during the day. There are more 15.................................. on main routes into the city, making it safer for the huge number of students and residents who rely on bicycles to get around. And 16.................................. public transport has helped to keep down the cost of using buses. Meanwhile, the police and the courts are coming down hard on drivers who misuse the roads, handing down large 17.................................. on selfish, inconsiderate drivers who believe it is their right to 18.................................. the roads.

Science & technology

1. Replace the words and phrases in bold in the sentences with a suitable alternative from the box.

advances	analysed	breakthrough	combined	cybernetics
development	discovered	experimented	genetic engineering	
innovations	invented	life expectancy	molecular biology	
nuclear engineering	proliferated	react	research	safeguards
a technophile	a technophobe			

1. The company is carrying out **scientific study** to find a cure for AIDS. ....

2. The **planning and production** of the new computer system will take some time. ....

3. Modern home entertainment systems and other **modern inventions** are changing everyone's lives. ....

4. Some elements **change their chemical composition** when mixed with water. ....

5. The scientists have **created** a new machine to automate the process. ....

6. Who was the person who **found** penicillin? ....

7. When the food was **examined closely and scientifically,** it was found to contain harmful bacteria. ....

8. Rain **joined together** with CO_2 gases produces acid rain. ....

9. Ron is **terrified of modern technology.** ....

10. Geoff is **very interested in modern technology.** ....

11. **Protection** against accidents in this laboratory are minimal. ....

12. The companies **performed scientific tests** with different types of glue before they found one that worked properly. ....

13. Brian is studying **the techniques used to change the genetic composition of a cell so as to change certain characteristics which can be inherited.** ....

14. Sarah is studying **the things which form the structure of living matter.** ....

15. Christine is studying **how information is communicated in machines and electronic devices in comparison with how it is communicated in the brain and nervous system.** ....

16. Neil is studying **the different ways of extracting and controlling energy from atomic particles.** ....

17. There has been a **sudden success** in the search for a cure for cancer. ....

18. **The number of years a person is likely to live** has increased a great deal thanks to modern medicine and technology. ....

19. The number of schools offering computer programming courses has **quickly increased** in the last ten years. ....

20. In spite of all the **progress** it has made in the last 50 years or so, medical science still knows little about the brain. ....

Science & technology

2. The person describing their computer in this passage is not very familiar with computer terminology. Replace the phrases in bold with more appropriate words and phrases from the box.

base unit	chat rooms	components	crashed	download	email
files	gaming	hardware	Internet	keyboard	laptop	load
log on	monitor	mouse	PC	printer	scanner	software	stream
virus	websites	wireless

OK, here's my new desktop **computer which has been designed to be used by just one person** (1).................................... . As you can see, it has five **parts which make up the whole thing** (2) .... Now, the **large box with the slots and sliding disc carrier** (3) .... is the most important part. It carries all the **stuff that makes the computer work** (4) .... You can also **put in** (5) .... your own games and other **programs used by computers for doing particular jobs** (6) ...., like photo processing and office suites. Next to it there is the **thing that looks like a small television** (7) .... so you can see what the computer is doing. To the right of that, there is the **machine that lets you make colour copies of the documents and other things that you create on the computer** (8) .... (this particular one incorporates a **machine you can use to copy pictures on to your computer, a bit like a photocopier** (9) ....). You control the computer using the **rectangular flat thing with all the letters and numbers on** (10) ...., or the **object with the little wheel on the top which you can move across the desk** (11) .... These usually have a lead connecting them to the computer, but as you can see, mine is **not physically connected to the computer, and instead sends electronic signals through the air** (12) ....

It's a very useful machine, of course. Once you **start using it by entering a password** (13) .... ,you can create **information that you store under a particular name** (14) .... and documents, **move** (15) .... pictures from your camera and, well, loads of things really. The best thing, however, is that you can access the **thing that links computers from around the world** (16) .... You can check out millions of **special computer pages created by companies, organisations and individuals all over the world** (17) ...., go shopping, play games (I really enjoy **playing games on my computer** (18) ....), **play** (19) .... music and videos, and **send electronic letters to** (20) .... your friends and family. It's also great for contacting people using **online places where people communicate with each other in real time** (21) .... and other social networking sites.

Unfortunately, I can't let you use it at the moment because it **stopped working** (22) .... at the weekend, and I can't get it to work again. I'm rather worried that it's got a **technical fault that someone created on purpose to affect my computer** (23) .... However, you can have a go on my **small computer that I can carry around with me** (24) .... if you like. If I can find it. The last time I remember seeing it was last night on the bus, when I was coming home from my office at the Ministry of Defence.

3 Now look at this essay and fill in the gaps with one of the words or phrases from Exercises 1 and 2. In some cases, more than one answer will be possible. You may need to change some of the word forms.

'Technology has come a long way in the last 50 years, and our lives have become better as a result. Or have they?'

The last 50 years have seen more changes than in the previous 200. There have been many remarkable advances in medicine and medical technology that have helped to increase our average 1...................................... way beyond that of our ancestors. Incredible 2...................................... such as satellite television have changed the way we spend our leisure hours. Perhaps the most important 3...................................... , however, has been the microchip. Nobody could have imagined, when it was first 4...................................... , that within a matter of years, this tiny piece of silicon and circuitry would be found in almost every household object from the kettle to the video recorder. And nobody could have predicted the sudden proliferation of computers that would completely change our lives, allowing us to access information from the other side of the world via the 5...................................... or send messages around the world by 6...................................... at the touch of a button. Meanwhile, 7...................................... into other aspects of information technology is making it easier and cheaper for us to talk to friends and relations around the world. Good news for 8...................................... who love modern technology, bad news for the 9...................................... who would prefer to hide from these modern miracles.

But everything has a price. The development of 10...................................... led to mass automation in factories, which in turn led to millions losing their jobs. The genius of Einstein led indirectly to the threat of nuclear war and the dangerous uncertainties of 11........................... (we hear of accidents and mishaps at nuclear power stations around the world, where 12...................................... to prevent accidents were inadequate). The relatively new science of 13...................................... has been seen as a major step forward, but putting modified foods on to the market before scientists had properly 14...................................... them was perhaps one of the most irresponsible decisions of the 1990s. Meanwhile, pharmaceutical companies continue to 15...................................... on animals, a move that many consider to be cruel and unnecessary.

Of course we all rely on modern science and technology to improve our lives. However, we need to make sure that we can control it before it controls us.

Sport

1 Look at the definitions, and arrange the letters in bold to make the words they are defining. Write your answers in the grid (the first letter of each word is already in place). If you do this correctly, you will reveal another word in the shaded vertical strip.

1   Someone who watches a public activity or event, especially a sports event. **pateorsct**

2   Money given to an organisation to help pay for something, often an event. **soriponpshs**

3   A man who plays sport. **mastsnopr**

4   To be involved in an activity with other people. **atek rpta ni**

5   To start doing something regularly as a habit, job or interest. **etka pu**

6   A person, team, business or group that someone is competing against. **popitioons**

7   A large building, usually without a roof, where people play and watch sports events. **utismad**

8   To win against someone in a game, fight or election. **efetda**

9   Someone who likes to watch a particular sports team, and wants that team to win. **potesprru**

10 A large building, usually with a roof, where sports events take place in a central area. **raane**

11 Someone who plays a sport or does an activity as a job rather than for enjoyment. **nesprsioalof**

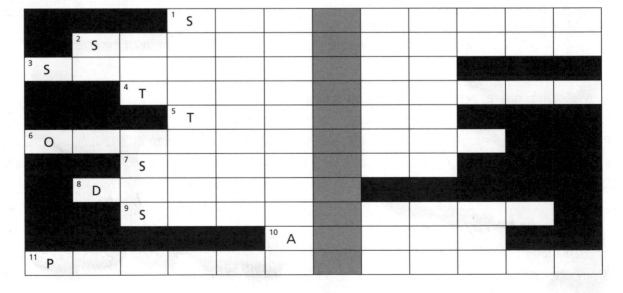

2 Imagine that you are a professional sports player and keen spectator. How would you feel in the following situations, happy (☺) or unhappy (☹)?

1.   Your team has been **promoted**.   ☺   ☹

2.   You are sent off during a game.   ☺   ☹

3.   Someone believes you have been taking **performance-enhancing drugs**.   ☺   ☹

4.   People say you are **grossly overpaid**.   ☺   ☹

5.   Your team has **reached the final**.   ☺   ☹

6.   In a 100 metre race, you **beat your personal best**.   ☺   ☹

7. You have been **disqualified** from taking part in a competition. ☺ ☹

8. You have failed a **dope test**. ☺ ☹

9. Your team has been **relegated**. ☺ ☹

10. Your country's national football team **qualifies** for the World Cup. ☺ ☹

11. Your feel that your team has no **team spirit**. ☺ ☹

12. There are a lot of **hooligans** at a match you attend. ☺ ☹

13. In a cycling race, you **outdistance** the other competitors. ☺ ☹

14. People say you are always **committing professional fouls**. ☺ ☹

15. When you walk on to the pitch to play a game, the spectators start **jeering**, **booing** and **shouting abuse**. ☺ ☹

16. The spectators **cheer** when you walk on to the pitch. ☺ ☹

17. You **outplay** your opponent in a game of squash. ☺ ☹

18. A newspaper article accuses you of **match fixing**. ☺ ☹

3 Complete this passage with words and phrases from Exercises 1 and 2. In some cases, more than one answer is possible, and you will need to change some of the word forms.

For many people, football is more than just a game. Whether they're (1) .... on the terraces, (2) .... on their favourite team, or whether they're (3) .... players (4) .... a major match, football is a way of life. They could not conceive of a world in which the 'beautiful game' does not exist. For them, nothing can match that magical moment when their team (5) .... for a major competition like the World Cup, (6) .... then (7) .... the opposition in a resounding victory. And, apart from seeing their team lose, nothing can be worse for them than seeing their favourite team (8) .... at the end of the season: to see your team moved down from the first division can be a heartbreaking experience. Anyone who has ever been inside a (9) .... during a major match can testify to the passion people have for the game.

However, there is an ugly side to football. It only takes a few (10) .... throwing bottles, invading the pitch and (11) .... at the players to ruin a match. This has been a problem for a long time, but evidence suggests that it is getting worse. There is criticism, too, that many top players are (12) .... People cannot understand how they can justify their huge salaries simply for kicking a ball around a pitch. They get even angrier when these extremely wealthy young men are caught using (13) ...., or are (14) .... in disgrace during a match for (15) .... against other players. There is also the more recent problem of (16) .... committed by players, coaches, officials and corrupt referees. Acting dishonestly to get the result you want not only goes against the spirit of the game, people say, but also gives the game a bad reputation.

Town & country

1 Match the sentences in the left-hand column with the most appropriate sentence in the right-hand column. Use the words and phrases in bold to help you.

1. London is a truly *cosmopolitan* city.

2. A modern *metropolis* needs a good integrated transport system.

3. London suffers a lot from traffic *congestion.*

4. *Poverty* in the *inner-city* areas can *breed crime.*

5. Cities around the world have seen a huge *population explosion.*

6. Birmingham has plenty of *amenities.*

7. A lot of people visit Paris for its *cultural events.*

8. Cities in poorer countries often lack basic *infrastructures.*

9. The *pressures of modern city life* can be difficult to deal with.

10. The *cost of living* in some places can be very high.

11. A lot of people appreciate the *anonymity* of living in a large city.

12. I love the *urban lifestyle* I lead.

13. In Singapore, private cars are banned from the *central business district* at *peak periods.*

14. *Urban sprawl* is prevalent in most cities.

A. *Drug abuse* is also a big problem.

B. Shops, libraries, hospitals and entertainment complexes are just a few of them.

C. Chief among these are concerts and exhibitions.

D. In particular, I enjoy the *atmosphere* that is unique to the city.

E. Prices in London are particularly exorbitant.

F. Without them, they are unable to function properly as cities.

G. It is especially bad during the *rush hour,* when thousands of *commuters* try to enter or leave the city.

H. Stress-related illnesses are very common in cities like New York.

I. Nowadays there are more *city dwellers* than ever before.

J. Everywhere you go there are *building sites, pedestrian precincts, blocks of flats* and *housing estates* spreading into the countryside.

K. They like to feel that they can do something without everybody knowing about it.

L. Most people use buses and the underground to get to the banks and offices where they work.

M. Unfortunately, this is something that most large capital cities lack.

N. It's a *melting pot* for people from all parts of the world.

2 Match the sentences in the left-hand column with an appropriate response in the right-hand column. Use the words and phrases in bold to help you.

1. I enjoy a *rural* lifestyle.	A. Really? So why are we seeing so much *construction* in the countryside around London?
2. There isn't much *pollution* if you live outside a town.	B. I'm not so sure. All those *pesticides* and *chemical fertilisers* that farmers use nowadays can't be good for the *environment.*
3. There is a lot of *productive land* in this area.	C. That's probably because we import more food from abroad.
4. In recent years, there has been a lot of *migration* from the towns to the cities.	D. Mostly *wheat, oats* and *barley.*
5. The government has promised to leave the green belt alone.	E. Really? How much is that in *acres*?
6. There has been a huge reduction in the amount of *arable land* over the last 20 years.	F. I'm not surprised. With such terrible *prospects* within towns, *depopulation* is inevitable.
7. My uncle's farm covers almost 800 *hectares.*	G. Well I can't see much evidence of *cultivation.*
8. What are the main *crops* grown in this area?	H. Do you? I always find there's nothing to do in the countryside.

3 Complete this article with words and phrases from Exercises 1 and 2. In some cases, more than one answer is possible.

For seven years I lived in Singapore, a 1...................................... of almost three million people. Like London, Paris and New York, Singapore is a 2...................................... city, with people from different parts of the world living and working together. I enjoyed the 3...................................... lifestyle I led there, and made the most of the superb 4...................................... , ranging from the excellent shops to some of the best restaurants in the world. In the evenings and at weekends there were always 5...................................... ; with such diverse attractions as classical western music, an exhibition of Malay art or a Chinese opera in the street, it was difficult to get bored. Perhaps most impressive, however, was the remarkable transport 6...................................... , with excellent roads, a swift and efficient bus service and a state-of-the-art underground system which could whisk 7...................................... from the suburbs straight into the heart of the city (this was particularly important, as the government banned private cars from entering the 8...................................... during the morning and afternoon 9...................................... in order to reduce 10...................................... on the roads and 11...................................... from the exhausts).

Of course, living in a city like this has its disadvantages as well. For a start, the 12...................................... can be very high – renting an apartment, for example, is very expensive. And as the city is expanding, there are a lot of 13...................................... where new apartments are continually being built to deal with the 14...................................... which is a direct result of the government encouraging people to have more children.

Fortunately, Singapore doesn't suffer from problems that are common in many cities such as 15...................................... , which is partly the result of the government imposing very severe penalties on anyone bringing narcotics into the country, so it is safe to walk the streets at night. In fact, the 16...................................... housing estates there are probably the safest and most orderly in the world.

Singapore wouldn't be ideal for everyone, however, especially if you come from the countryside and are used to a 17...................................... lifestyle. The traditional villages that were once common have disappeared as the residents there realised there were no 18...................................... for their future and moved into new government housing in the city. Nowadays, there is very little 19...................................... around the city, which means that Singapore imports almost all of its food. And despite a 'green' approach to city planning, the 20...................................... which has eaten into the countryside has had a detrimental effect on the 21...................................... .

Travel

1 Look at the following sentences and decide if they are true or false. If they are false, explain why.

1. A *travel agency* is the same as a *tour operator.* **True / False**

2. A *package tour* is a holiday in which the price includes flights, transfers to and from the airport and accommodation. **True / False**

3. An *all-inclusive* holiday is a holiday in which the price includes flights, transfers, accommodation, food and drink. **True / False**

4. When passengers *embark,* they get *off* an aeroplane or ship. **True / False**

5. When passengers *disembark,* they get *on* an aeroplane or ship. **True / False**

6. The first thing you do when you go to an airport is go to the *check-in*. **True / False**

7. The first thing you do when you arrive at your hotel is *check in.* **True / False**

8. The opposite of a *package tourist* is an *independent traveller.* **True / False**

9. *Mass tourism* can have a negative effect on the environment. **True / False**

10. *Ecotourism* is tourism which has a negative effect on the environment. **True / False**

11. The words *trip, excursion, journey* and *voyage* all have the same meaning. **True / False**

12. It is always necessary to have a *visa* when you visit a different country. **True / False**

13. A flight from London to Paris could be described as a *long-haul* flight. **True / False**

14. Flying *economy class* is more expensive than flying *business class*. **True / False**

15. A Canadian citizen flying from Toronto to Vancouver will have to fill in an *immigration card* before she arrives. **True / False**

16. *Cultural tourism* is the same as *sustainable tourism*. **True / False**

17. The *peak season* is the time of the year when many people are taking their holiday. **True / False**

18. A *cruise* is a holiday where you go somewhere (usually Africa) to watch and take photographs of wild animals **True / False**

19. An *armchair traveller* is someone who books holidays and flights on the Internet. **True / False**

20. A *tourist trap* is a place that is visited by many tourists and is therefore crowded and expensive. **True / False**

2 Complete the sentences with a suitable word or phrase from the box.

> border controls   culture shock   deported   economic migrants
> emigration   expatriates   immigration   internally displaced
> persona non grata   refugees   repatriated   UNHCR

1. At the beginning of the war, thousands of .... fled over the border to the next country.

2. Since the civil war began, almost a million people have been forced to move to another part of the country. These .... persons are now without food or shelter.

3. Nineteenth century governments encouraged .... to the colonies.

4. The government is encouraging .... because of the shortage of workers in key industries.

5. Moving from a large European city to the small village in the Himalayas was something of a ....

6. Thousands of British .... live in the Gulf States, where many of them have high-powered jobs.

7. The .... is under a lot of pressure owing to the huge number of displaced persons around the world.

8. He was .... from the country when his visa expired.

9. Because he had a criminal record, the government didn't want him to enter the country, declared him .... and asked him to leave immediately.

10. After the economy collapsed in the east, thousands of .... headed west in the hope of finding a good job.

11. People who are caught trying to enter the country illegally are usually held in a detention centre before being ....

12. .... were tightened in order to reduce the number of people illegally entering the country.

3 Now look at this essay and complete the gaps with one of the words or phrases from Exercises 1 and 2. In some cases, more than one answer may be possible. You will need to change the form of some of the words.

'Travel: the other side of the coin'

Most of us have, at some point in our lives, experienced the joys of travel. We go to a 1.. to pick up some brochures, or look on the Internet for a cheap holiday deal. We book a two-week 2.. with flights and accommodation included (or if we are 3.. , we make our own way to the country and travel around from place to place with a rucksack on our back). We make sure we have all the right currency, our passport and any 4.. that are necessary to get us into the country. We go to the airport and 5.. . We strap ourselves into our tiny 6.. aircraft seats and a few hours later we 7.. from the aircraft, strange new sights, smells and sounds greeting us. Nowadays, it seems, the whole world goes on holiday at once: the age of 8.. is in full swing!

But for the great majority of people around the world, travel for them is done in the face of great adversity and hardship. They never get to indulge in an 9.. holiday in a luxury hotel with all meals and drinks included. They never get to explore the lush Amazon Rain Forest or the frozen wastes of the Arctic on an 10.. holiday. For them, travel is a matter of life and death. I refer, of course, to all the 11.. escaping from their own countries, or the 12.. , moved from one part of their country to another by an uncaring government, or 13.. forced to find a job and seek a living wherever they can.

Can you imagine anything worse than the misery these people must face? Let's not confuse them with those 14.. who choose to live in another country and often have nice houses and high salaries. These people are simply desperate to survive. As well as losing their homes because of war or famine or other natural disasters, they must come to terms with their new environment: for many, the 15.. can be too great. And while many countries with an open policy on 16.. will welcome them in with open arms, others will simply turn them away. These people become 17.. , unwanted and unwelcome. Even if they manage to get into a country, they will often be 18.. or repatriated. Their future is uncertain.

Something to think about, perhaps, the next time you are 19.. to your five-star hotel by a palm-fringed beach or sitting in a coach on an 20.. to a pretty castle in the countryside.

Work

1 How would you generally feel, happy 🙂 or unhappy 🙁, if you were in the following situations? Use the words and phrases in bold to help you decide.

1. The company you work for is well known for its *job security.* 🙂 🙁

2. You are suddenly *made redundant.* 🙂 🙁

3. You receive a *promotion.* 🙂 🙁

4. You are given an *increment.* 🙂 🙁

5. You work *unsociable hours.* 🙂 🙁

6. You have a *steady job.* 🙂 🙁

7. You had *adverse working conditions.* 🙂 🙁

8. You suddenly find yourself *unemployed.* 🙂 🙁

9. You need time off work because of *repetitive strain injury.* 🙂 🙁

10. The office where you work has *sick building syndrome.* 🙂 🙁

11. You receive regular *perks* as part of your job. 🙂 🙁

12. Somebody calls you a *workaholic.* 🙂 🙁

13. Your company gives you plenty of *incentives.* 🙂 🙁

14. Your boss announces that there is going to be some *downsizing* of the workforce. 🙂 🙁

15. You have a lot of *job satisfaction.* 🙂 🙁

16. Your company has a generous *incentive scheme.* 🙂 🙁

17. You receive a *commission* for the work you have done. 🙂 🙁

18. You receive support from a *union.* 🙂 🙁

19. You are under *stress.* 🙂 🙁

20. You are forced to *resign.* 🙂 🙁

21. You receive a *cut* in your *salary.* 🙂 🙁

22. Your company gives you *sickness benefit.* 🙂 🙁

23. You find your job very *demanding.* 🙂 🙁

24. Your boss tells you that you have *potential*. 🙂 🙁

25. Your boss tells you that you *lack initiative* and *motivation*. 🙂 🙁

26. Everyone at work *ignores* you. 🙂 🙁

2 Match sentences 1 – 6 in box A with one of the sentences A – F in box B. Write the person's name after each sentence A – F. Use the words and phrases in bold to help you.

Box A.

1. Samantha is the assistant manager of a bank and she works from 8.30 to 5.30 every day.

2. Tracy works on the production line of a factory which makes cars. She uses a machine to spray paint on to the finished car parts.

3. Jane works for herself. She is a photographer. She works every day for about eight or nine hours.

4. Jeanette is a cleaner for a company in Birmingham, but she only works there for about three or four hours a day.

5. Claire has a powerful job in the personnel office of a large multinational company. She is responsible for employing new people and getting rid of those that the company doesn't want to employ any more.

6. Marie works in the finance department of an international college in Oxford.

Box B.

A. She is a *semi-skilled blue-collar worker* in a *manufacturing industry*. ....

B. She is *self-employed* and works *full-time.* She likes to describe herself as *freelance*. ....

C. She is responsible for *hiring and firing.* ....

D. She calculates the *wages, salaries, pension contributions* and *medical insurance contributions* of all the staff. ....

E. She is a *full-time white-collar worker* in a *service industry.* ....

F. She is an *unskilled part-time employee*. ....

Work

3 Now read this essay and complete the gaps with one of the words or phrases from Exercises 1 and 2. You will need to change the form of some of the words.

'Some people live to work, and others work to live. In most cases, this depends on the job they have and the conditions under which they are employed. In your opinion, what are the elements that make a job worthwhile?'

In answering this question, I would like to look first at the elements that combine to make a job undesirable. By avoiding such factors, potential 1.. are more likely to find a job that is more worthwhile, and by doing so, hope to achieve happiness in their work.

First of all, it doesn't matter if you are an 2.. worker cleaning the floor, a 3.. 4.. worker on a production line in one of the 5.. , or a 6.. worker in a bank, shop or one of the other 7.. : if you lack 8.. , with the knowledge that you might lose your job at any time, you will never feel happy. Everybody would like a 9.. in which he or she is guaranteed work. Nowadays, however, companies have a high turnover of staff, 10.. new staff and 11.. others on a weekly basis. Such companies are not popular with their workers.

The same can be said of a job in which you are put under a lot of 12.. and worry, a job which is so 13.. that it takes over your life, a job where you work 14.. and so never get to see your family or friends, or a physical job in which you do the same thing every day and end up with the industrial disease that is always in the papers nowadays – 15.. .

With all these negative factors, it would be difficult to believe that there are any elements that make a job worthwhile. Money is, of course, the prime motivator, and everybody wants a good 16.. . But of course that is not all. The chance of 17.. , of being given a better position in a company, is a motivating factor. Likewise, 18.. such as a free lunch or a company car, an 19.. scheme to make you work hard such as a regular 20.. above the rate of inflation, 21.. in case you fall ill and a company 22.. scheme so that you have some money when you retire all combine to make a job worthwhile.

Unfortunately, it is not always easy to find all of these. There is, however, an alternative. Forget the office and the factory floor, become 23.. and work for yourself. Your future may not be secure, but at least you will be happy.

Page 1 Addition, equation & conclusion

1

Addition	Equation	Conclusion
and along with also as well as besides furthermore in addition moreover too what's more	equally correspondingly in the same way likewise similarly	in conclusion in brief therefore thus to conclude to summarise to sum up briefly we can conclude that

2

1. Furthermore / In addition / In Moreover / What's more (this is less formal than the other expressions),   2. As well as / Besides (not In addition, as this would need to before the verb),   3. Likewise / Similarly / In the same way (the main verb in both sentences is the same (respect), so we can use a word / phrase of equation here),   4. As well as / Along with,   5. Also / Furthermore / In addition / Moreover / What's more,   6. Likewise / similarly,   7. Likewise / In the same way / Similarly,   8. In brief,   9. In brief / We can conclude that,   10. Therefore (to sum up, to conclude and to summarise are usually used to conclude a longer piece of writing. Thus is slightly more formal than therefore, but has the same meaning)

Page 2 Around the world

1

1. the Far East,   2. Antarctic (Antarctica is the name of the continent, and is not preceded by the),   3. Australasia,   4. the Indian subcontinent,   5. Central America,   6. Latin America,   7. southern Africa (South Africa is the name of a country),   8. the United Kingdom,   9. Europe,   10. the Gulf States,   11. Scandinavia,   12. capital (Traditionally, a capital city is the city in a country where the government is based. Cities which are larger than the capital cities of a country, for example, Istanbul, are often known as principal cities)

2

1. Afghan,   2. Argentine,   3. Australian,   4. Bangladeshi,   5. Belgian,   6. Brazilian,   7. Canadian,   8. Danish,   9. Egyptian,   10. English / British,   11. Finnish,   12. Greek,   13. Indian,   14. Iranian,   15. Iraqi,   16. Irish,   17. Israeli,   18. Japanese,   19. Kuwaiti,   20. Lebanese,   21. Malay / Malaysian,   22. Mexican,   23. Moroccan,   24. Dutch,   25. Norwegian,   26. Pakistani,   27. Peruvian,   28. Filipino,   29. Polish,   30. Portuguese,   31. Russian,   32. Saudi Arabian,   33. Scottish / British,   34. Spanish,   35. Swedish,   36. Swiss,   37. Thai,   38. Turkish,   39. Welsh / British,   40. Yemeni

Pages 3 – 4 Changes 1

⇒ The words and phrases in this module are particularly useful for Part 1 of the IELTS Writing Test, where you may be asked to write about changes shown in tables or graphs.

1

1. increased / rose / went up (in any order),   2. fell / dropped / went down / declined (in any order),   3. remained steady / remained constant (in either order),   4. fluctuated / peaked at / reached a peak of (in either order)

2

1. gradually / steadily (in either order),   2. slightly,   3. dramatically / sharply (in either order),   4. upward trend

3

The number of visitors to Seahaven (1) increased / rose / went up (2) gradually / steadily between April and June, then (3) increased / rose / went up (4) dramatically / sharply in July, and continued to (5) go up / increase / rise in August. For the first four months, visitor numbers to Bridgeport (6) fluctuated, but then (7) dropped / fell / declined / decreased / went down (8) dramatically / sharply

Answers

in the final month. Westhampton visitor numbers (9) *remained constant / remained steady* from April to June, then (10) *increased / rose / went up* (11) *slightly* in July and finally (12) *peaked at / reached a peak of* 11,000 in August.

Overall, there was an (13) *upward trend* in the number of visitors to Seahaven and Westhampton, but a (14) *downward trend* in the number of people visiting Bridgeport.

(Remember to vary your vocabulary in Writing tasks. Try not to use the same word too often. If, for example, you use *increase* in one part, use *rise* in another, and *go up* in another.)

Pages 5 – 6 Changes 2

1

1. altered /alter,   2. switching / switched,   3. adjust / adjust,   4. faded / faded,   5. varies / vary,   6. reduce / reduce,   7. deteriorate / deteriorated (we can also say *worsen* or *get worse*),   8. swell / swells,   9. exchanged / exchange,   10. renovate / renovate

2

1. replaced / replace,   2. adapt / adapted,   3. disappear / disappeared,   4. promoted / promoted,   5. relax / relax,   6. improve / improving,   7. expand / expanded,   8. cut / cutting,   9. transformed / transformed,   10. declined / declining

Page 7 Condition

1

1. providing that* you return,   2. provided that* I have,   3. unless you get (*unless* means the same as *if you don't*),   4. on condition that* they tidy (*on condition that* is quite formal),   5. as long as we continue,   6. no matter how much you,   7. however many books you,   8. wherever you

* We can omit *that* after *providing*, *provided* and *on condition*. We can also use *the* before *condition*.

Note: All of these sentences can also <u>begin</u> with the conditional word or phrase. For example: *You can borrow my dictionary providing that you return it before you go home* = *Providing that you return it before you go home, you can borrow my dictionary*. When we do this, we are shifting the emphasis of the sentence to the conditional clause.

Pages 8 – 9 Confusing words & false friends 1

1. abroad / aboard,   2. action / activity,   3. advise / advice,   4. effect / affect,   5. appreciable / appreciative,   6. prevent / avoid,   7. beside / Besides,   8. Shortly / briefly,   9. canal / channel,   10. conscious / Conscientious,   11. considerate / considerable,   12. continual / continuous,   13. control / inspect,   14. objection / criticism,   15. injury / harm / damage,   16. for / while / during,   17. However / Moreover,   18. wounded / injured

Pages 10 – 11 Confusing words & false friends 2

1. job / work,   2. lie / lay,   3. watch / look at,   4. lose / loose,   5. make / cause,   6. nature / countryside,   7. per cent (often written as one word: *percent*) / percentage,   8. permit / permission,   9. personal / personnel,   10. possibility / chance,   11. practise / practice (note that in American English, *practi̱ce* is both a noun and a verb),   12. Priceless / worthless,   13. principle / Principal / principal / principle,   14. trouble / problem,   15. procession / process,   16. rise / raise,   17. remember / remind,   18. respectful / respectable,   19. tolerant / tolerable,   20. treat / cure

Other confusing words or false friends include:
actually + now, already + yet, afraid of + worried about, bring + fetch, conduct + direct, discover + invent, driver + chauffeur, formidable + wonderful, fun + funny, go + play (for sports and games), come along with + follow, kind + sympathetic, lend + borrow, overcome + overtake, pass + take (an exam), receipt + recipe, scenery + view, sensible + sensitive, special + especially, take + bring

Pages 12 – 13 Context & meaning 1

1

2 (suggested answers). *nocturnal*: active at night rather than during the day. / *cites*: mentions something as an example or explanation of something else. / *coherently*: spoken or written so that all the different parts fit together, and / or which are easy to understand. / *feat*: something impressive that someone does.

3
(a) burden, (b) prolific, (c) initiative, (d) resilient, (e) sways, (f) elusive, (g) implement, (h) arduous, (i) fringe, (j) prohibitive, (k) exhaustive, (l) forage, (m) stacks, (n) imperative, (o) mediocre

Remember that some words can have a different meaning depending on their context. For example, *prohibitive* can also mean *limiting something, or preventing something from being done* (e.g., *prohibitive anti-piracy laws*).

In addition to looking at the *context* in which a word appears in order to work out its meaning, you should also identify its *function* (is it a noun, verb, adjective, adverb, etc?). Some of the words in Exercise 2 can have a different function without changing their form, depending on how they are used (e.g., *burden* can be a verb as well as a noun).

Pages 14 – 15 Context & meaning 2

1
1. Incorrect (stop someone or something from making progress or developing), 2. Correct, 3. Incorrect (speak publicly to a group of people), 4. Incorrect (badly built or made, and so likely to break easily), 5. Correct, 6. Incorrect (become a full member of a group or society), 7. Incorrect (the start of something), 8. Incorrect (inventing or using new ideas), 9. Incorrect (gradually becomes narrower towards one end), 10. Correct, 11. Incorrect (nice to look at), 12. Correct

2
1. Incorrect (rough and hard), 2. Incorrect (spread ideas, beliefs, etc., to a lot of people), 3. Correct, 4. Incorrect (able to be done, or worth doing), 5. Incorrect (believe or say that something was written, said, painted, etc, by a particular person), 6. Incorrect (an official document that, among other things, prevents someone from copying someone else's invention), 7. Correct, 8. Incorrect (to be reasonable or necessary), 9. Correct, 10. Incorrect (connected with something, but not a necessary or important part of it), 11. Incorrect (to make or persuade somebody to do something), 12. Incorrect (had changes made in order to improve it)

Pages 16 – 17 Context & meaning 3

1
1. infancy: the time when you are a baby or very young child.
2. personnel: the people who work for a company or organisation.
3. prolong: to make something last longer.
4. windswept: having a lot of wind, and not many buildings or trees to protect it.
5. threefold: three times as much, or three times as many (also written *three-fold*. Other numbers can be used: *twofold*, *tenfold*, etc.).
6. scholars: people who study a particular subject and know a lot about it, especially if the subject is not scientific.
7. recipient: (formal) someone who receives something.
8. centrepiece: the most important object or decoration in a particular place.
9. multitude: a very large number of things or people.
10. numeracy: basic skills in mathematics.
11. lifespan: the length of time that an animal or human lives.
12. monetary: consisting of money, or able to be measured in money.
13. grandeur: an impressive quality that a place, object or occasion has.
14. standpoint: a way of considering something from someone's point of view.

2
1. epicentre: the area of land directly over the centre of an earthquake.
2. outpatients: people who receive medical treatment at a hospital, but do not stay there for the night.
3. validate: to officially prove that something is true or correct.
4. widespread: happening or existing in many places, or affecting many people.
5. seafarers: people who work or travel regularly on the sea, especially sailors.
6. spatial: relating to the size, shape and position of things (the 'root' word is *space*).
7. monorail: a railway system in which trains travel on a single metal track.
8. auditory: relating to hearing.
9. industrious: always working very hard.

Answers

10. longevity: having a long life or existence.
11. drawback: a feature of something that makes it less useful than it could be.
12. showcases: shows someone or something in a way that attracts attention and emphasises their good qualities.
13. wilderness: an area of land where people do not live or grow crops, and where there are no buildings.
14. illiterate: unable to read or write.

Page 18 Contrast & comparison

1. A, 2. B, 3. B, 4. C (*differentiate* and *distinguish* have exactly the same meaning), 5. C, 6. A, 7. C, 8. A, 9. B, 10. C, 11. A, 12. C, 13. C, 14. B, 15. B (this is an informal expression)

Page 19 Emphasis & misunderstanding

1
1. F, 2. B, 3. E, 4. C, 5. A, 6. D

2
1. accentuated / emphasised, 2. prominent, 3. accent / emphasis / stress, 4. put great stress, 5. crucially important / extremely important / of crucial importance, 6. emphasis

3
1. confused, 2. confusion, 3. mix-up (this is an informal word), 4. obscure, 5. misapprehension, 6. assumed, 7. mistaken, 8. impression

Page 20 Focusing attention

1
1. simply, 2. largely, 3. primarily, 4. mainly, 5. exclusively, 6. particularly, 7. specifically, 8. notably, 9. mostly, 10. purely, 11. chiefly

The word in the bold vertical box is *principally*.

2
Only or solely: simply, exclusively, purely, specifically

In most cases, normally, or the main reason for something: chiefly, largely, mainly, mostly, notably, particularly, primarily.

Pages 21 – 22 Generalisations & specifics

1
1. D, 2. A, 3. B, 4. H, 5. L, 6. E, 7. O, 8. F, 9. I, 10. J, 11. N, 12. M, 13. G, 14. C, 15. K

2
Specific things: the specifics, characteristics, details, exemplifies, illustrate, illustration, itemise, minutiae, peculiar to, peculiarity, technicality

General things: generalisations, outline, gist, in general

Other words and phrases you might find useful include:
for the most part, generalities, in general terms, on the whole, to generalise, list (as a verb), specify

Page 23 Groups

1
People in general: crowd, gang, group, huddle, throng
A group of people working together: cast, company, crew, platoon, staff, team
Animals: flock, herd, litter, pack, shoal (of fish. We can also say *school*), swarm*
Objects: batch**, bunch, bundle, pile (we can also say *heap*), set, stack

* swarm can also be used informally for a large group of people (*Swarms of police officers surrounded the building*)

** *batch* can also be used to talk about a number of people that arrive or are dealt with at the same time (*This new batch of students seems very nice*)

2
1. herd, 2. cast, 3. swarms, 4. piles / stacks / heaps, 5. shoals / schools, 6. crew, 7. set, 8. staff,
9. bunch, 10. crowd / throng (or, more informally, *swarm*), 11. packs, 12. group / huddle,
13. flocks, 14. batch, 15. bundle, 16. gangs / crowds / groups

---

Page 24 How something works

⇨ *The words and phrases in this module are particularly useful for the IELTS Listening Test (where you may hear someone describing how something works) or Part 1 of the IELTS Writing Test (where you may be shown a picture or diagram of something, and have to explain how it works).*

1. A thermostat
A thermostat *contains* a strip or coil of steel and a strip or coil of copper, one on top of the other. As the strip / coil **heats up**, the metals **expand**, but one does it faster than the other. The strip / coil **bends** and **connects** with a switch, which **turns off** the power supply. When the strip / coil **cools down**, the metals **contract** and the switch is **disconnected**. The thermostat is **adjusted** using a dial or other control.

2. A disc player
A disc player (for example, in a computer) has several component parts. A disc is **inserted** into the player and begins to **spin**. At the same time, a thin beam of light called a laser **strikes** the disc and **converts** digital signals into sounds or images, which can be **heard** through speakers or **viewed** on a screen. Volume or brightness can be **increased** or **decreased** by means of a button, knob or other control. Nowadays, discs are largely being **replaced** by storage devices like memory sticks, which have no moving parts.

3. An aerosol
In an aerosol, liquid and gas are **compressed** in a metal and / or hard plastic tube. This can be **released** from the tube by **pushing** a button, which **opens** a valve. When the liquid–gas combination **leaves** the tube and **mixes** with oxygen, it rapidly **expands**.

4. An aircraft
Most aircraft are **made** of aluminium, and require two forces to allow them to fly: thrust and lift. As the aircraft **moves** forward on the ground under the power of its engines, air **flows** over the wings. As it **accelerates / moves** faster, **creating / producing** more thrust, a vacuum is **created / formed** over the wings. This **creates / produces** lift. The aircraft is **pulled** into the air by the force of this lift.

5. A digital camera
A digital camera **consists** of two main parts: a body and a lens. When a button is **pressed** on the body, a window in the lens called a *shutter* **opens** and light **enters** the camera. The amount of light going into the camera is **controlled** by both the speed of this shutter, and a smaller window called an *aperture*. Both the shutter speed and the size of the aperture can be **adjusted** by the person using the camera. The light **hits** a sensor in the body of the camera, which **records** the light as a digital image. The image is **recorded / stored** on a memory card in the camera, and this can later be **downloaded** onto a computer.

Other words and phrases you might find useful include:
fold, reflect, reverse, revolve, start, stop, turn, turn down, turn up, unfold, unwind, upload, wind

Note: When we describe how an object works and there is no other person or agent involved in our description, we use the *active voice* ('…light *enters* the camera…', '…the metals *expand*…'). When there is a person involved in the process, we usually use the *passive voice* (*is / are* + a past participle: 'The thermostat *is adjusted*…', '…liquid and gas *are compressed*…'). We use the passive voice when we do not know who does the action or process, or because we do not need to say who does it.

Page 25 Joining / becoming part of something bigger

1
1. linked, 2. amalgamated / merged, 3. blended, 4. merged / amalgamated, 5. incorporated,
6. integrated / assimilated, 7. assimilated / integrated, 8. took over / swallowed up (*swallowed up* is less formal than *took over*. We can also say *acquired*), 9. got together (an informal phrase. We can also say *met* or *assembled*, which are slightly less informal), 10. took over / swallowed up

Answers

2

1. alliance, 2. union, 3. federation, 4. alloy, 5. compound, 6. synthesis, 7. unification,
8. blend, 9. coalition, 10. merger

Page 26 Likes & dislikes

1

1. Positive, 2. Positive, 3. Negative, 4. Positive, 5. Negative, 6. Negative, 7. Negative,
8. Positive (*fancies* in this context is an informal way of saying *would like to*), 9. Positive,
10. Positive, 11. Positive, 12. Positive, 13. Negative, 14. Positive, 15. Positive, 16. Negative,
17. Positive, 18. Positive

attract, *captivate*, *disgust*, *fascinate*, *repel* and *tempt* can be active (*New technology <u>fascinates</u> me*),
but are more commonly passive (*I <u>am fascinated by</u> new technology*)

Pages 27 – 29 Location & direction

⇨ *Language of location and direction is particularly useful for the IELTS Listening Test, where you
may be asked to locate places or other things on maps or plans.*

1

1. directly opposite, 2. to the west of, 3. on the south side of, 4. to the east of, 5. on the
left-hand side of (we can just say *on the left side of*), 6. in the middle of, 7. halfway along (we can
also say *halfway up*), 8. parallel to, 9. at right angles to (when something is at a 90° angle to
something else, we can also say that it is *perpendicular to* it), 10. on the north side of, 11. halfway
between, 12. diagonally opposite, 13. surrounded by, 14. on, 15. on the corner of

2

You are going to A (the hotel)

Note: A *crossroads* is a place where one road crosses another. A crossroads is a type of *junction*
(a place where one road crosses or joins another). The American word is *intersection*).

3

<u>To the supermarket</u>
1. Go to the end, 2. turn right, 3. take the first, 4. on your left, 5. second / last, 6. on your left

<u>To the language school</u>
7. Go along, 8. turn right, 9. crossroads, 10. Take the first, 11. on your left, 12. first,
13. on your right

<u>To the book shop</u>
14. Go along, 15. turn left, 16. crossroads, 17. the end, 18. turn left, 19. take the second,
20. on your right, 21. Go past, 22. last, 23. on your right

Pages 30 – 31 Modified words

1

1. teleconferences, 2. biannual (something that is *biannual* occurs twice a year, something that is
biennial occurs once every two years*), 3. autobiography, 4. transformed, 5. predetermined,
6. semi-final (this can also be written as one word, *semifinal*, or two words, *semi final*),
7. postgraduate, 8. co-workers, 9. micro-organisms (this can also be written as one word,
microorganisms, or two words, *micro organisms*), 10. unisex, 11. substandard,
12. circumnavigate, 13. International, 14. monolingual, 15. underachiever, 16. overpopulated

* Rather confusingly, something that is *biweekly* occurs twice a week *or* once every two weeks
(e.g., *A biweekly newsletter*). Something that is *bimonthly* occurs twice a month *or* once every two
months (e.g., *a bimonthly meeting*).

2

1. microwaves, 2. telecommunications, 3. unilateral, 4. semi-detached, 5. autopilot,
6. bilingual, 7. circumvented, 8. post-war (this can also be written as one word, *postwar*),
9. premature, 10. overweight, 11. subconscious, 12. coeducational (we can also write this
co-educational), 13. underestimated, 14. transatlantic (note that *Atlantic* does not begin with a
capital letter in this word, but would need to when used on its own), 15. interrelationship,
16. monotone

Answers

Pages 32 – 33 Objects & actions

1

1. freeze,　2. spin,　3. slide,　4. evaporate,　5. congeal (for blood, we would say *clot*),　6. rotate,　7. wobble,　8. leak (we could also say *escape*. The noise it makes is a *hiss*),　9. vibrate (if the glass is loose in the frame, it would also *rattle*),　10. fade,　11. rise,　12. erode,　13. smoulder,　14. expand,　15. stretch,　16. crack (if the glass breaks completely, it *shatters*),　17. spill,　18. explode

2

1. revolve,　2. subside,　3. flow,　4. melt,　5. bounce,　6. grow,　7. set,　8. condense,　9. meander,　10. spread,　11. trickle (if the water is coming out very slowly in small drops, we say *drip*),　12. burn,　13. crumble,　14. contract,　15. ring (we also use this word for the noise a telephone makes when someone is calling you),　16. sink,　17. float,　18. erupt

3

1. froze,　2. float,　3. rising,　4. fades,　5. condense,　6. subsided,　7. revolved,　8. set,　9. trickle,　10. stretched,　11. bounce (we can also *bounce ideas around*. These are informal expressions),　12. leaked

Page 34 Obligation & option

1

1. False (you must take your own pencil and eraser),　2. True,　3. False (he had to pay the money back),　4. False (they don't have to pay any income tax at all),　5. True,　6. False (the companies *make* them work long hours: the employees have no choice),　7. True,　8. False (you can attend the classes if you want to),　9. False (you *must* wear a crash helmet. We can also use the word *obligatory*),　10. True

2

1. obliged / required,　2. no alternative,　3. liable for,　4. compulsory,　5. voluntary,　6. mandatory,　7. required,　8. force,　9. optional,　10. exempt

Pages 35 – 36 Opinion, attitude & belief

1

1. tolerance,　2. obsessed,　3. reckon (this is quite an informal word),　4. suspect,　5. bigoted,　6. doubt,　7. fanatical,　8. dedicated,　9. opinion,　10. pragmatic,　11. committed,　12. regarding,　13. disapproval,　14. maintain,　15. concerned,　16. cynical,　17. exception,　18. convinced,　19. traditional,　20. conservative

2

1. suspicious,　2. pragmatic,　3. fanatical,　4. disapprove,　5. opinion,　6. dedication / commitment,　7. tolerate,　8. conservative / traditional,　9. doubt,　10. maintain / reckon / suspect / doubt

Page 37 Opposites: adjectives

1. clear,　2. easy,　3. graceful,　4. detrimental,　5. approximate,　6. innocent,　7. even,　8. scarce,　9. flexible,　10. marked,　11. crude,　12. delicate,　13. dim,　14. obligatory (we can also say *compulsory*),　15. reluctant,　16. widespread,　17. costly,　18. chronic

Page 38 Opposites: verbs

1. accepted,　2. denied,　3. retreating,　4. agreed,　5. defended,　6. demolished,　7. simplified,　8. abandon,　9. deteriorated,　10. Rewarding,　11. lowered,　12. forbidden,　13. fell,　14. loosen,　15. withdrew,　16. retained,　17. accelerates,　18. ignored

Page 39 Ownership, giving, lending & borrowing

1

1. landlords (*landlady* = female. We can also say *landowner*),　2. Proprietors / Owners,　3. owners,　4. property,　5. estate / property,　6. possessions,　7. belongings (*possessions* usually refers to everything we own, for example, our homes, furniture, etc. *Belongings* usually refers to smaller things, for example, briefcase, mobile phone, etc.),　8. loan,　9. mortgage,　10. tenants,　11. rent,　12. donation

Mortgage, *rent* and *loan* can also be verbs.

Answers

2
1. lend,   2. hire,   3. borrow,   4. ✓,   5. present,   6. ✓,   7. allocate,   8. provide

Page 40 Phrasal verbs 1

1. up,   2. out,   3. up to,   4. off,   5. on,   6. up with,   7. down,   8. out of,   9. out,   10. out,   11. up,   12. in,   13. up with,   14. out,   15. out,   16. into,   17. on,   18. behind,   19. down / back on,   20. out,   21. over,   22. with,   23. forward,   24. back on

Pages 41 – 42 Phrasal verbs 2

1. broke down,   2. work out,   3. wear off,   4. wear … out,   5. pull through,   6. sort out,   7. split up,   8. showed up,   9. pulled out of,   10. letting off,   11. let … down,   12. carry on,   13. held up,   14. fell through,   15. ended up,   16. carried out,   17. cutting back on,   18. cut off,   19. did away with,   20. do up

Page 43 Phrasal verbs 3

1. looked,   2. get,   3. getting,   4. looking,   5. go,   6. look,   7. get,   8. go,   9. came,   10. give,   11. look,   12. go,   13. went,   14. go,   15. look,   16. come / get,   17. comes,   18. looked / went,   19. get,   20. came

Pages 44 – 45 Phrasal verbs 4

<u>Clues across</u>
1. put down,   4. talk…round,   5. take after,   6. running up against,   8. turned out,   11. picked on,   12. opt out,   16. turned up,   19. set off,   20. run up,   21. made up

<u>Clues down</u>
1. put aside (*set aside* has the same meaning, but does not fit in the crossword),   2. take in,   3. taken in,   5. turned down,   7. put up with,   9. stand in (also used with *for*: *I was asked to <u>stand in for</u> him*),   10. put off,   13. sets in,   14. make out,   15. made up,   17. ran for,   18. pick up

Page 46 Presenting an argument

⇨ *You will find the words and phrases in this module useful in Part 2 of the IELTS Writing Test, and also in the Speaking Test (especially Part 3, where you are asked to talk about a topic and say what you think about it).*

1. However,   2. First of all / Firstly,   3. As well as / In addition to,   4. I believe / I think,   5. Moreover / Furthermore,   6. Although / While,   7. as well,   8. Nevertheless,   9. The most important reason / The main reason,   10. As far as I am concerned / For me,   11. Many consider,   12. Secondly,   13. Finally,   14. In other words,   15. In conclusion / To summarise,   16. On the one hand,   17. On the other hand,   18. In my opinion

Note: The sample answer is longer than you would need to write in the IELTS.

When you are asked to present an argument, you should always look at it from two sides, giving reasons why you agree and / or disagree before reaching a conclusion. It is usually best to present your argument in favour of something just before the conclusion.

Page 47 Reason & result

1
1. The police asked him his reason for speeding through the town,   2. He failed his exam due to / on account of / owing to (these phrases have the same meaning as *because of*) his lack of revision,   3. A persistent cough prompted him to seek professional medical help,   4. She started haranguing the crowd with the aim of starting a riot,   5. He spent the whole weekend revising in order to pass his exams,   6. They came in quietly so as not to wake anyone,   7. He refused to lend anyone money on the grounds that people rarely repay a loan,   8. The bank manager refused to lend the company more money on account of / due to / owing to its low turnover and poor sales history,   9. The school was forced to close due to / on account of / owing to poor student attendance,   10. What were your motives for upsetting me like that?,   11. What are the effects of a large earthquake,   12. Stress and overwork can affect different people in different ways,   13. The army attacked without considering the consequences of / effects of its action,   14. He failed to send off his application form and as a

consequence was unable to enrol for the course (*as a consequence* has the same meaning as *as a result*),   15. Riots and street fighting ensued when the police officers on trial were acquitted.

2

1. ensued,   2. consequence of / effects of,   3. in order to,   4. with the aim of,   5. on account of / due to / owing to,   6. reason for,   7. prompted him to,   8. on the grounds that,   9. so as not to,   10. affect

---

Page 48 Shape & feature

1

1. a pyramid,   2. a spiral,   3. a circle,   4. an oval,   5. a triangle,   6. a cube,   7. a sphere,   8. a crescent,   9. a square,   10. a cylinder,   11. a rectangle,   12. a cone

2

1. circular,   2. rectangular,   3. oval,   4. spiral,   5. spherical,   6. triangular,   7. conical,   8. cylindrical,   9. square

For words like pyramid, crescent and cube, we add –shaped (*a pyramid-shaped building, a cube-shaped container*)

3

1. (d),   2. (g),   3. (i),   4. (h),   5. (j),   6. (b),   7. (e),   8. (a),   9. (c),   10. (f)

Pages 49 – 50 Size, quantity & dimension

1

1. small (note the pronunciation of *minute* in this sense: / mal'nju:t /),   2. small,   3. big,   4. big (this is an informal use of the word *mammoth*),   5. big,   6. big,   7. big,   8. small,   9. big (this is an informal use of the word *monumental*),   10. big,   11. big,   12. big (this is an informal use of the word *loads*),   13. small,   14. big,   15. big,   16. big,   17. big,   18. big,   19. big, 20. big,   21. small,   22. big,   23. big,   24. big (this is an informal use of the word *tons*),   25. big

2

1. a long-distance journey,   2. a great deal of time,   3. loads of times,   4. a minute amount of dust,   5. a gigantic wave,   6. a huge waste of time,   7. A colossal statue,   8. plenty of food,   9. A broad river,   10. A vast crowd of supporters,   11. a gargantuan meal / plenty of food,   12. a vast room,   13. a mammoth job / tons of work,   14. a deep lake,   15. a minuscule piece of cloth,   16. an enormous book,   17. a mammoth job / tons of work,   18. a high mountain,   19. a monumental error,   20. a tiny car,   21. a giant building,   22. a wide avenue,   23. a shallow pool,   24. a tall man,   25. A narrow alleyway

---

Page 51 Spelling

The incorrectly-spelt words are <u>underlined</u> and corrected below.

1

Despite banning tobacco <u>advertising</u> and <u>raising</u> the price of <u>cigarettes</u>, the <u>government's</u> anti-smoking <u>campaign</u> has failed to have any long-term <u>effects</u>. It is now widely <u>believed</u> that more drastic measures are <u>necessary</u>. A new national <u>committee</u>, which has been formed to tackle the <u>problem</u>, has made several <u>recommendations</u>. These include banning smoking in all public areas, and denying hospital treatment to <u>persistent</u> smokers who have been warned by their doctors to give up but failed to do so.

2

It is <u>arguable</u> <u>whether</u> good <u>pronunciation</u> is more important than good <u>grammar</u> and <u>vocabulary</u>. <u>Conscientious</u> students balance their <u>acquisition</u> of these skills, <u>hoping</u> to <u>achieve</u> both fluency and <u>accuracy</u>. English teachers should encourage <u>their</u> students to practise all the relevant language skills, and use their English at every <u>opportunity</u>.

3

It is <u>becoming</u> increasingly <u>difficult</u> for many people to find decent <u>accommodation</u> in the city at a price they can afford. To put it <u>simply</u>, there are <u>too</u> many people and not enough homes for them. Local <u>community</u> centres and charitable <u>organisations</u> such as *Home Front* can offer <u>advice</u>, but it is widely agreed that the situation is no longer <u>manageable</u>. The fact that some councils in the city

Answers

are building cheap, <u>temporary</u> housing for lower-paid <u>professionals</u> is the only official <u>acknowledgement</u> of this problem.

Page 52 Stopping something

1. delete, 2. repeal (we can also say *abolish*), 3. deter, 4. dissuade, 5. rescind, 6. suppress, 7. sever, 8. turn down (we can also say *decline*), 9. pull out of, 10. deny, 11. cancel, 12. quash, 13. give up, 14. put an end to, 15. remove (less formally, we can say *strike*, but only if we are referring to something on paper: *Strike his name from the list*), 16. suspend, 17. scrap, 18. curb

Page 53 Success & failure

1. reached, 2. accomplish, 3. secured, 4. achieved, 5. realise, 6. attain, 7. fulfilled, 8. managed*, 9. abandon, 10. collapsed, 11. faltered, 12. folded, 13. fell through, 14. misfired

* We *manage <u>to do</u>* something, or we *succeed <u>in doing</u>* something (*He <u>managed to pass</u> his exam* / *He <u>succeeded in passing</u> his exam*).

Page 54 Task commands

1
1. F, 2. D, 3. C, 4. H, 5. A, 6. G, 7. B, 8. E

2
1. D, 2. G, 3. A, 4. H, 5. E, 6. B, 7. C

Other words and phrases which you might find useful include:
calculate, characterise, classify, comment on, consider, deduce, describe, determine, differentiate between, distinguish between, evaluate, explain, give an account of, identify, list, show, state, summarise

Page 55 Time

1
<u>Part 1:</u>
1. Prior to (this phrase is usually followed by a noun or by an -ing verb. For example: *Prior to moving to the country, he had to learn the language*), 2. By the time, 3. Formerly (we could also use *Previously*, but *Formerly* works better in this context), 4. precede, 5. Previously. 6. Earlier (we could also use *Previously*)

<u>Part 2:</u>
1. While (we can also say *As* or *Just as*. Note that *while* is usually used to talk about long actions. For short actions, we would use *when*), 2. During (we can also say *Throughout*. *During* and *throughout* are followed by a noun), 3. In the meantime, 4. At that very moment

<u>Part 3:</u>
1. Following (this word is always followed by a noun. We can also say *After*), 2. As soon as (we can also say *Once* or *The moment / minute that*. These words and phrases are always followed by an action: *Once the show had ended, we went home*), 3. Afterwards

2
(1) <u>In the past</u>: a few decades ago, at that point / moment in history, at the turn of the century, back in the 1990s, between 2003 and 2005, from 2006 to 2011, in medieval times (note that *medieval* can also be spelt *mediaeval*), in my childhood / youth, in those days, last century
(2) <u>The past leading to the present</u>: ever since, for the past few months, lately, over the past six weeks
(3) <u>The present</u>: as things stand, nowadays, these days
(4) <u>The future</u>: by the end of this year, for the foreseeable future, for the next few weeks, from now on, in another five years' time, one day, over the coming weeks and months, sooner or later

1

<u>Agreeing with somebody:</u> I agree. / I couldn't agree more. / That's just what I think. / That's my view exactly. / That's right.

<u>Disagreeing with somebody:</u> I don't entirely agree. / I'm afraid I disagree / don't agree. / I see things rather differently myself. / Well, actually… / Well, as a matter of fact,…

<u>Interrupting somebody:</u> Could I just say that…? / Excuse me for interrupting,… / Let me interrupt you there. / Sorry to butt in,… / Sorry to interrupt,… (*You shouldn't interrupt the examiner too often. In any case, the examiner will leave you to do most of the talking*)

<u>Asking somebody for their opinion:</u> Do you agree that…? / What are your feelings about…? / What are your views on…? / What do you think about…? / What's your opinion? (*You probably won't need to use these expressions yourself in the Speaking Test, but you are likely to hear the examiner use them*)

2

<u>Asking for clarification or repetition:</u> Could you repeat the question? / I'm afraid I didn't catch that. / I'm sorry? / What was that? / Would you mind repeating that?

<u>Saying something in another way:</u> In other words… / Perhaps I should make that clearer by saying… / To put it another way,… / What I'm trying to say is… / What I mean is…

<u>Giving yourself time to think:</u> Hmm, how can I put / say this? / Let me see. / Let me think about that for a moment. / May I think about that for a moment? / That's an interesting question.

<u>Summing up what you have said:</u> So, basically,… / In short / brief,… / So, in conclusion,… / To summarise,… / To sum up,…

3

1. Any expression from the 'Asking for clarification or repetition' box.
2. Any expression from the 'Agreeing with somebody' box.
3. Any expression from the 'Interrupting somebody' box except *Could I just say that…?* (which would be used before giving an opinion rather than correcting a mistake, as the student is doing here).
4. Any expression from the 'Giving yourself time to think' box except *May I think about that for a moment?* (which would require a response from the interviewer before the student continues).
5. Any expression from the 'Saying something in another way' box.
6. Any expression from the 'Disagreeing with somebody' box.

Pages 58 – 60 Architecture

1

Building materials: concrete, glass, reinforced concrete, steel, stone, timber

Aesthetic perception: controversial, elegant, an eyesore, pleasing geometric forms, ugly, well-designed

Types of building: high-rise apartments (in the UK, the word *flat* is usually used instead of *apartment*), low-rise apartments, multi-storey car park, skyscraper

Architectural style: art deco, international style, modernist, post-modern, standardised, traditional (*high-tech* could also be included in this category)

Parts of a building: foundations, façade, porch, walls

Features: energy-efficient, functional, high-tech, practical

2

1. B, 2. A, 3. C, 4. C, 5. A, 6. A, 7. C, 8. C, 9. A, 10. A, 11. B, 12. A (we can also say *loft*)

3

1. planning, 2. preservation, 3. renovate, 4. architects, 5. glass, 6. façade, 7. foundations, 8. social, 9. derelict, 10. estate, 11. an eyesore, 12. traditional, 13. slums, 14. high-rise / low-rise, 15. energy-efficient

Other words and phrases which you might find useful include:

Other types of building: bungalow, castle, cottage, detached house, maisonette, manor house, mansion, palace, semi-detached house, shopping centre / mall, terraced house

Other parts of a building: basement / cellar, chimney, roof, staircase, walls

Verbs: construct, design, modernise, plan

Others: development, low-cost, mass-produced, prefabricated, standardised

Answers

Pages 61 – 63 The arts

1

1. a ballet, 2. a play, 3. a biography, 4. a sculpture, 5. a portrait, 6. an opera, 7. a concert, 8. a novel, 9. a collection of short stories, 10. a still life, 11. photography, 12. a film, 13. abstract art, 14. a landscape

2

1. performance, 2. works (or *work*), 3. edition, 4. reviews (a *revue* is a type of performance with songs, dances and humour), 5. exhibition (an *exhibit* in the context of art is an object that forms part of an exhibition), 6. grant, 7. Gallery (a *galley* is a type of ship or a kitchen on a ship or plane), 8. novelists (we can also say *writers*), 9. Impressionists (*Impressionism* is the style of painting), 10. publish, 11. atmospheric, 12. artistic, 13. popular, 14. cinematic, 15. Surrealist (the noun is *Surrealism*), 16. cultural

3

1. ballet, 2. performance, 3. reviews, 4. exhibition, 5. Gallery, 6. portraits, 7. still life, 8. grant, 9. novelist, 10. works / novels, 11. published, 12. biography, 13. concert, 14. opera, 15. sculpture

Other words and phrases which you might find useful include:
actor, artist, author, collection, exhibit, pop art, production, produce, sculptor

Pages 64 – 66 Business & industry

1

1. demand for, 2. loss, 3. net, 4. lending, 5. credit, 6. retail, 7. private, 8. State-owned industries, 9. Unskilled labourers, 10. take on (we can also say *employ* or *hire*), 11. White-collar, 12. exports, 13. recession, 14. employees (we can also say *staff* or *workers*), 15. expenditure, 16. shop floor (*…a fight broke out <u>on</u> the shop floor.* In this context, the *shop floor* is the area in a factory where products are made. This phrase can also be used to mean the workers in a factory, not the managers)

2

A. interest rates, B. secondary industries, C. GNP (= Gross National Product), D. output, E. primary industry, F. automation, G. service industries, H. balance of payments, I. deficit, J. monopoly, K. nationalised industries, L. unemployment, M. taxation, N. key industries, O. inflation, P. income tax, Q. VAT (= Value Added Tax), R. salary

3

1. Interest, 2. borrowing, 3. lay off, 4. unemployment, 5. Inflation, 6. exports, 7. secondary industries, 8. Blue-collar / White-collar, 9. state-owned / nationalised, 10. salaries, 11. management, 12. public, 13. Demand, 14. supply, 15. revenue / income, 16. nationalised, 17. deficit, 18. automation

Pages 67 – 68 Children & the family

1

1. nuclear, 2. extended, 3. single-parent, 4. bring up (we can also say *raise* or *rear*), 5. upbringing, 6. divorced, 7. childcare, 8. adolescence (the noun is *adolescent*), 9. formative years, 10. birth rate, 11. dependants (the adjective is *dependent*), 12. Juvenile

2

1. H (*authoritarian* can also be a noun: *a strict authoritarian*), 2. C, 3. G, 4. K, 5. A, 6. D, 7. J, 8. B, 9. E, 10. F, 11. I, 12. L

3

1. formative, 2. divorced, 3. brought up, 4. foster family (a child who lives with a foster family is a *foster child*), 5. authoritarian, 6. upbringing, 7. running wild, 8. adolescence, 9. juvenile, 10. responsible, 11. siblings, 12. well-adjusted, 13. lenient, 14. over-protective, 15. nuclear, 16. single-parent, 17. dependants, 18. extended

Pages 69 – 70 Crime & the law

1

1. judge, 2. jury, 3. witness, 4. defendant, 5. victim, 6. solicitor (called an *attorney* in the US), 7. offender, 8. barrister, 9. law abiding, 10. break the law

2

Part 1 (in order): A, F, D, B, C, E

Part 2 (in order): A, E, F, C, B, D

Part 3 (in order): A, D, F, C, E, B

3

1. committed, 2. arrested / charged, 3. court, 4. pleaded, 5. guilty, 6. sentenced, 7. misdeeds, 8. law-abiding / innocent, 9. retribution, 10. rehabilitate, 11. reform, 12. released, 13. deterrent, 14. parole, 15. victim, 16. offender, 17. community service, 18. fine, 19. + 20. corporal punishment / capital punishment (in either order), 21. + 22. judges / barristers / juries / solicitors (any of these in any order)

Other words and phrases you might find useful include:
accuse, admit, convict (noun + verb), conviction, deny, lawyer, pass a verdict, punish, punishment, revenge, send to prison, statement, wrongdoer

Different types of crime (and the people who commit them): bigamy (a bigamist), burglary (a burglar), espionage (a spy), forgery (a forger), hijack (a hijacker), hooliganism (a hooligan), murder (a murderer), piracy (a pirate), rape (a rapist), robbery (a robber), shoplifting (a shoplifter), terrorism (a terrorist), vandalism (a vandal)

Pages 71 – 72 Education

1

1. A (we can also say *retake*), 2. B, 3. B, 4. C, 5. C, 6. A, 7. C, 8. B, 9. B, 10. C, 11. B, 12. A, 13. B, 14. A

2

1. kindergarten (we can also say *nursery* or *nursery school*), 2. primary, 3. skills, 4. + 5. numeracy / literacy (in either order), 6. secondary, 7. discipline, 8. passed (The opposite of *pass* is *fail*), 9. course, 10. enrolled, 11. graduated (this can also be a noun: *a graduate*. A graduate is a student who has finished a course at university. A student who is still at university is called an *undergraduate*), 12. degree, 13. on-line, 14. qualifications, 15. day release, 16. evening class

3

1. skills, 2. + 3. literacy / numeracy (in either order), 4. kindergarten, 5. primary, 6. secondary, 7. discipline, 8. pass, 9. qualifications, 10. acquire, 11. health, 12. further, 13. enrol, 14. higher, 15. graduate, 16. degree, 17. higher, 18. evening class, 19. day release, 20. on-line, 21. mature 22. graduate

Other words and phrases which you might find useful include:
adult education, campus, co-educational, comprehensive school, faculty, infant school, junior school, private education, resources, subject, take / sit an exam

Pages 73 – 74 The environment

1

1. F (the opposite of an animal which has been raised on a battery farm is a *free-range* animal, e.g., a *free-range chicken*. Eggs can also be described as free-range: *I only eat free-range eggs*), 2. L, 3. J (some of these animals are called *protected species*, which means it is usually illegal to kill them), 4. E, 5. B, 6. C, 7. D, 8. K, 9. I, 10. G, 11. H, 12. A (we can also say *hunting*, although there are some differences. Poaching means to *hunt illegally*)

2

1. green belt, 2. biodegradable packaging, 3. greenhouse, 4. rain forest (often written as one word, *rainforest*), 5. erosion, 6. recycle, 7. organic, 8. genetically modified (often abbreviated to *GM*), 9. Deforestation, 10. Acid rain, 11. ecosystem, 12. emissions + fossil fuels, 13. contaminated (we can also say *polluted*), 14. environmentalists, 15. global warming

Answers

3

1. fossil fuels, 2. acid rain, 3. greenhouse, 4. global warming, 5. rain forest, 6. contaminated, 7. emissions / gases, 8. Poaching, 9. endangered species, 10. ecosystem, 11. recycle, 12. biodegradable, 13. genetically modified, 14. organic, 15. pollution, 16. environmentalists, 17. conservation programmes, 18. battery farming, 19. green belts

Other words and phrases which you might find useful include:
bottle bank, carbon dioxide, CFC gases, climatic change, degradation, destruction, energy-efficient, the greenhouse effect, legislation, over-fishing, overpopulation, the ozone layer, radioactive waste, recycling facilities, re-use, rising sea levels, toxic waste, waste disposal

---

Pages 75 – 77 Food & diet

1

1. vitamins, 2. nutritious (the noun is *nutrition* (general) or *nutrient* (specific). A person who specialises in the study of nutrition and advises on diets is called a *nutritionist*), 3. vegetarian (this word can also be an adjective: *a vegetarian diet*), 4. carbohydrates, 5. protein, 6. cholesterol, 7. famine, 8. obesity (the adjective is *obese*), 9. malnourished (the noun is *malnutrition*), 10. minerals, 11. fat, 12. fibre (*digest* = change into substances your body can use), 13. overweight, 14. fresh, 15. calories (the adjective is *calorific*: *What is the calorific content of a bar of chocolate?*), 16. processed (the chemicals and other things in processed food are called *additives*)

2

1. I (the noun for *allergic* is *allergy*. Some people also have a food *intolerance*, which means they cannot digest certain foods properly: *James has an intolerance to wheat*), 2. C, 3. A, 4. J or D, 5. D or J, 6. E, 7. B, 8. G, 9. H, 10. F (fast food is also often called *junk food*)

3

1. fast food, 2. processed, 3. vitamins / minerals, 4. minerals / vitamins, 5. fat / carbohydrates, 6. carbohydrates / fat, 7. obesity, 8. malnourished, 9. shortages, 10. harvest, 11. cholesterol, 12. balanced diet, 13. fresh, 14. fibre

---

Pages 78 – 79 Geography

1

1. tree, copse, wood, forest (*beach* does not belong in this group)
2. footpath, track, lane, road (*peak* does not belong in this group)
3. hillock, hill, mountain, mountain range (*shore* does not belong in this group)
4. hollow, gorge, valley, plain (*waterfall* does not belong in this group)
5. inlet, cove, bay, gulf (*ridge* does not belong in this group)
6. brook, stream, river, estuary (*cliff* does not belong in this group)
7. city, county, country, continent (*tributary* does not belong in this group)
8. pond, lake, sea, ocean (*cape* does not belong in this group)

2

Geographical features associated with water and the sea:
beach, cape, cliff, coast, coastline, glacier, mouth (of a river), peninsula, shore, source (of a river), tributary, waterfall

Geographical features associated with land, hills and mountains:
cliff, glacier, highlands, mountainous, peak, plateau, ridge, summit

Words / phrases associated with agriculture and rural land:
depopulation, fertile, irrigation, under-developed, vegetation

Words / phrases associated with towns and cities:
conurbation, densely populated, industrialised, overcrowding, urban sprawl

3

1. densely populated, 2. industrialised, 3. urban sprawl, 4. city, 5. irrigation, 6. source, 7. peaks, 8. mountain range, 9. depopulation, 10. Valley, 11. waterfalls, 12. brooks / streams, 13. lane, 14. track, 15. Ocean, 16. cape / peninsula, 17. hills, 18. plain, 19. delta, 20. fertile, 21. shore / beach, 22. country

Pages 80 – 81 Global problems

1

1. B, 2. A, 3. B, 4. C, 5. A, 6. C, 7. A, 8. B, 9. A, 10. C, 11. B, 12. B, 13. A, 14. B, 15. A

Note: A *hurricane* is the name we give to a tropical storm with strong winds and rain which originates in the Caribbean or Eastern Pacific. Similar storms which originate in the Far East are called *typhoons*, and those which originate in the Indian Ocean are called *cyclones*.

2

1. spread, 2. spread / swept (in this context, *swept* is always followed by *through*), 3. erupted,
4. shook, 5. broke out, 6. casualties, 7. survivors / casualties, 8. Refugees / Survivors,
9. suffering, 10. relief

3

1. torrential, 2. flood, 3. epidemic, 4. famine, 5. relief, 6. volcano, 7. erupted, 8. hurricane,
9. devastation, 10. typhoon, 11. casualties, 12. drought, 13. civil war, 14. Refugees / Survivors,
15. swept / spread, 16. accident, 17. explosions, 18. plague

Pages 82 – 83 Healthcare

1

1. D, 2. H (a combination of 1 and 2 is called *rheumatoid arthritis*), 3. C, 4. A, 5. K, 6. B, 7. E,
8. L, 9. F (we can also say that their bodies lack *resistance to illness*), 10. I (The *National Health Service*, often abbreviated to *the NHS*, is a system of free doctors, nurses, hospitals and clinics supported by the government in the UK. Many people prefer *private healthcare* because it is generally considered to be more efficient), 11. J, 12. G

2

1. therapeutic (the noun is *therapy*. A person who provides a therapeutic service is called a *therapist*), 2. a diet (in this context, *diet* refers to the food we eat. If we *go on a diet*, we eat less in order to lose weight), 3. conventional medicine, 4. traditional medicines, 5. holistic medicine (an example of this is *aromatherapy*), 6. consultant (we can also say *specialist*), 7. surgeon (*surgery* is the treatment of disease which requires an operation to cut into or remove part of the body. Do not confuse this with *a surgery*, which is a room or building where a normal doctor* sees their patients),
8. protein, 9. vitamins, 10. minerals, 11. active (the opposite of this is *sedentary*: see Exercise 1),
12. welfare state (other features of the welfare state in the UK include providing citizens with adequate housing, education and money if they are unable to work)

* Called a *family doctor* or *general practitioner* (*GP*) in the UK.

3

1. welfare state, 2. + 3. cutbacks + underfunding (in either order), 4. conventional medicine,
5. traditional medicine, 6. arthritis, 7. consultant, 8. surgery, 9. therapeutic, 10. stress-related,
11. symptoms, 12. holistic medicine, 13. diet, 14. + 15. vitamins + minerals (in either order),
16. active, 17. sedentary, 18. arthritis / cancer / cardiovascular disease

Other words and phrases which you might find useful include:
blood pressure, consult, curable, cure, mental health, physical health, prescription, prevention, remedy, research, the World Health Organisation (the WHO)

Pages 84 – 85 The media

1

1. broadsheets, 2. tabloids, 3. journalists, 4. coverage (for radio and television, we often use the word *airtime*), 5. current affairs, 6. broadcasts, 7. log on, 8. reporters, 9. download, 10. the Internet, 11. information overload, 12. website

2

1. freedom of the press, 2. media tycoon (we can also say *media mogul* or *press baron**),
3. censorship, 4. unscrupulous, 5. exploiting, 6. invasion of privacy, 7. paparazzi,
8. + 9. information + entertainment (in either order), 10. chequebook journalism, 11. integrity,
12. investigative journalism, 13. readership, 14. gutter press, 15. libel

* This is informal and slightly negative, as it suggests the person has too much influence.

Answers

3

1. broadsheets, 2. coverage, 3. current affairs, 4. reporters, 5. journalists, 6. tabloids,
7. broadcasts, 8. the Internet, 9. websites, 10. download, 11. + 12. information + entertainment
(in either order), 13. gutter press / tabloids, 14. invasion of privacy, 15. paparazzi, 16. libel,
17. chequebook journalism, 18. unscrupulous, 19. integrity, 20. log on, 21. Media tycoons /
Journalists / Reporters, 22. censorship, 23. freedom of the press

Other words and expressions which you might find useful include:
Types of television programme: chat show, commercial**, documentary, drama, game show,
makeover show, quiz show, reality show, sitcom, soap opera, talent show, variety show, weather
forecast
Parts of a newspaper: advertisement**, colour supplement, editorial, entertainment, fashion,
financial, headline, horoscope, lead story, local news, national news, readers' letters (also called
letters to the editor), sport, what's on
Others: downmarket, highbrow, journal, lowbrow, read between the lines, slander, state-controlled,
tune in, upbeat, upmarket

** Television and radio stations show *commercials*, newspapers and magazines print *advertisements*.
However, the word *advertisements* (often shortened to *adverts* or, more informally, *ads*) is often
used instead of *commercials*.

Pages 86 – 88 Men & women

1

1. negative, 2. negative, 3. negative, 4. negative (a *glass ceiling* is an unfair system that prevents
some people, especially women, from reaching the most senior positions in a company or
organisation), 5. positive, 6. positive, 7. positive (if you are good at multi-tasking, you are good
at doing more than one thing at the same time), 8. negative (this could also be positive,
depending on your point of view), 9. negative, 10. negative, 11. negative (*unreconstructed* in
this context is a relatively new word, often used to describe a person, usually a man, who has
old-fashioned ideas, especially about women and their role), 12. negative (informal: in this
context, a *dinosaur* is someone who is very old-fashioned and no longer useful or effective),
13. positive, 14. positive, 15. negative

2

1. household management (we can also say *domestic chores* or *housework*), 2. practical, 3. male
counterparts, 4. Sex Discrimination Act (a British law which states that men and women should be
treated equally, with equal pay, terms and conditions for doing the same job, etc.), 5. child rearing,
6. role division, 7. breadwinner (we can also say *financial provider*), 8. social convention,
9. gender roles, 10. stereotypes, 11. battle of the sexes (a rather old-fashioned phrase which is
often used humorously)

3

1. egalitarian, 2. equality, 3. breadwinner, 4. weaker sex, 5. stereotypes, 6. gender roles,
7. male-dominated, 8. ruthless, 9. astute / versatile, 10. multi-tasking, 11. Sex Discrimination
Act, 12. male chauvinist, 13. unreconstructed, 14. glass ceiling, 15. role division, 16. child
rearing, 17. household management, 18. Social convention, 19. sex objects, 20. power struggle /
battle of the sexes, 21. male counterparts, 22. battle of the sexes / power struggle

Pages 89 – 90 Money & finance

1

1. **Profit** is the money you gain from selling something, which is more than the money you paid for
it. **Loss** is money you have spent and not got back.
2. **Extravagant** describes someone who spends a lot of money. **Frugal** describes someone who is
careful with money. **Economical** describes something that is not expensive to use or run.
3. A **current account** is a bank account from which you can take money at any time. A **deposit
account** is a bank account which pays you interest if you leave money in it for some time (we can
also say *savings account* or *notice account*).
4. A **loan** is money which you borrow to buy something. A **mortgage** is a special kind of loan used
to buy property (a house, a flat, etc.) over a period of time.
5. To **deposit** money is to put money into a bank account. To **withdraw** money is to take money out
of a bank account (*deposit* can be a noun or a verb. The noun of *withdraw* is *withdrawal*).

6. A **wage** and a **salary** are money you earn for doing a job, but a wage is usually paid daily or weekly, and a salary is usually paid monthly. We also use salary to describe the amount of money you earn over a year (*He earns an annual salary of £40,000*).

7. If you are **broke**, you have no money. This is an informal word. If you are **bankrupt**, you are not able to pay back money you have borrowed. This is a very serious financial situation for someone to be in.

8. In the UK, **shares** are one of the many equal parts into which a company's capital is divided. People who buy them are called *shareholders*. **Stocks** are shares which are issued by the government. **Dividends** are parts of a company's profits shared out among the shareholders.

9. **Income tax** is a tax on money earned as wages or a salary. **Excise duty** is a tax on certain goods produced in a country, such as cigarettes or alcohol.

10. To **credit** someone's bank account is to put money into the account. To **debit** someone's bank account is to take money out. In the UK, many people pay for telephone bills, etc., using a system called *direct debit*, where money is taken directly from their bank account by the company providing the goods or services.

11. Traditionally, a **bank** is a business organisation which keeps money for customers and pays it out on demand, or lends them money. A **building society** is more usually associated with saving money or lending people money to buy property. These days, there is very little difference between them.

12. A **discount** is the percentage by which a full price is reduced to a buyer by the seller. A **refund** is money paid back when, for example, returning something to a shop (it can also be a verb: *to refund*).

13. A **bargain** is something which is bought more cheaply than usual. Something which is **overpriced** is too expensive. Something which is **exorbitant** costs much more than its true value (*£12 for a cheese sandwich? That's exorbitant!*).

14. A **worthless** object is something which has no value. A **priceless** object is an extremely valuable object.

15. If you **save** money, you put it to one side so that you can use it later. If you **invest** money, you put it into property, shares, etc., so that it will increase in value.

16. **Inflation** is a state of economy where prices and wages increase. **Deflation** is a reduction in economic activity.

17. **Income** is the money you receive for doing something. **Expenditure** is the money you spend.

18. If you **lend** money, you let someone use your money for a certain period of time. If you **borrow** money from someone, you take money for a time, usually paying interest (*Can you lend me £20 until the end of the month?*).

2
1. F, 2. I, 3. L, 4. E, 5. J, 6. K (*Revenue and Customs* – full name: *Her Majesty's Revenue and Customs*, abbreviated to *HMRC* – is the British government department that deals with taxes), 7. C, 8. H, 9. G, 10. A, 11. B, 12. D

3
1. borrow, 2. loan, 3. income, 4. expenditure, 5. overdraft, 6. cost of living, 7. Inflation, 8. economise, 9. building society, 10. interest, 11. on credit, 12. exorbitant, 13. save, 14. reductions, 15. bargain, 16. discount, 17. invest, 18. stocks, 19. shares

Other words and phrases which you might find useful include:
cash, cheque, corporation tax, credit card, currency, debit card, debt, disability allowance, equity, inheritance tax, investment, negative equity, overdrawn, rate of exchange (or *exchange rate*), receipt, social security, statement, upwardly / downwardly mobile, wealthy

---

Pages 91 – 92 On the road

1
1. A, 2. B, 3. B, 4. A, 5. A, 6. B, 7. A, 8. A, 9. A, 10. A, 11. A, 12. A

2.
1. D, 2. H, 3. F, 4. A, 5. J, 6. G, 7. C, 8. I, 9. E, 10. B

Notes:
Most large towns and cities in the UK have 'Park and Ride' schemes. These are large car parks outside city centres where drivers can park their cars, often for free. They can then take a bus into the city centre.

Answers

Distances and speed limits in the UK are in *miles* (1 mile = about 1.6 kilometres) and *miles per hour* (*mph*). The maximum speed limit is 60mph on single-lane roads outside towns, or 70mph on dual carriageways and motorways (although this may increase to 80mph on motorways in the near future). In most built-up areas, the maximum speed limit is usually 20 or 30mph. Drivers who are caught speeding can face penalties ranging from a fine to imprisonment, depending on how fast they were driving and where. They also receive 'penalty points' on their driving licence, and can have their licence suspended.

Drink-driving is considered a serious offence. Offenders automatically have their driving licence suspended for at least a year, will normally receive a fine and in extreme cases (especially where they cause an accident), may go to prison.

3
1. + 2. injuries + fatalities (in either order),   3. speeding,   4. drink-driving,   5. pedestrians,
6. pedestrian crossings,   7. Highway Code,   8. + 9. congestion + pollution (in either order),
10. black spot,   11. transport strategy,   12. Traffic calming,   13. Park and Ride,   14. traffic-free zone,   15. cycle lanes,   16. subsidised,   17. fines,   18. dominate

Other words and phrases which you might find useful include:
Objects in the street: bollard, contraflow, crossroads, junction, kerb, pelican crossing, pavement, speed camera, traffic cones, traffic island, traffic lights, zebra crossing

Others: accelerate, brake, carriageway, central reservation, cut in, hard shoulder, highway, motorway, overtake, skid, slip road, swerve, tailgate

Pages 93 – 95 Science & technology

1
1. research,   2. development,   3. innovations,   4. react,   5. invented,   6. discovered,   7. analysed,
8. combined,   9. a technophobe,   10. a technophile (informally called a *techie*),   11. safeguards,
12. experimented,   13. genetic engineering,   14. molecular biology,   15. cybernetics,   16. nuclear engineering,   17. breakthrough,   18. Life expectancy,   19. proliferated,   20. advances

2
1. PC (= *personal computer*),   2. components,   3. base unit (we can also say *hard drive* or *disc* drive*),   4. hardware,   5. load (we can also say *install*),   6. software,   7. monitor,   8. printer,
9. scanner,   10. keyboard,   11. mouse,   12. wireless,   13. log on,   14. files,   15. download,
16. Internet,   17. websites,   18. gaming,   19. stream,   20. email (this word can also be a noun: *send an email*. It can also be written with a hyphen: *e-mail***),   21. chat rooms,   22. crashed,   23. virus,
24. laptop (we can also say *notebook*. Smaller laptops are called *netbooks*. Small computers which you control using your fingers or a tool like a pen are called *tablet PCs*)

* Also often spelt *disk*

** The letter *e* in *email* means **electronic**, and is used as a prefix for many things connected with computers, the Internet and modern technology: *e-book*, *e-commerce*, *e-learning*, *e-reader*, *e-shopping*, *e-ticket*, etc.

3
1. invented,   2. life expectancy,   3. innovations,   4. breakthrough,   5. invented,   6. Internet,   7. email,   8. research,   9. technophiles,   10. technophobes,   11. cybernetics,   12. nuclear engineering,
13. safeguards,   14. genetic engineering,   15. analysed,   16. experiment

Pages 96 – 97 Sport

1
1. spectator,   2. sponsorship (the people or organisations who provide the money are called *sponsors*. The verb is *to sponsor*),   3. sportsman (a woman who plays sport is a *sportswoman*),   4. take part in,
5. take up,   6. opposition,   7. stadium*,   8. defeat (often used in the passive voice to describe the losing team or player: *Once again, Chelsea have been beaten in the final*. We can also say *beat*),   9. supporter (The verb is *to support*. We can also say *fan*, which can be used for other things as well, including music groups, film stars, etc.,   10. arena**,   11. professional (this can be an adjective or a noun)

* Important football matches, baseball matches, etc., are often played on a *pitch* in a *stadium*.

** Important basketball matches, volleyball matches, etc., are often played on a *court* in an *arena*.

Answers

The word in the shaded vertical column is *competitors* (= the sportsmen and sportswomen who take part in a sports competition).

2

1. ☺, 2. ☹, 3. ☹, 4. ☹, 5. ☺, 6. ☺, 7. ☹, 8. ☹, 9. ☹, 10. ☺, 11. ☹, 12. ☹, 13. ☺, 14. ☹, 15. ☹, 16. ☺, 17. ☺, 18. ☹

3

1. spectators / supporters / fans, 2. cheering, 3. professional, 4. taking part in, 5. qualifies, 6. reaches the final, 7. defeats / beats, 8. relegated, 9. stadium, 10. hooligans, 11. shouting abuse / jeering, 12. grossly overpaid, 13. performance-enhancing drugs, 14. sent off, 15. committing professional fouls, 16. match fixing

Pages 98 – 99 Town & country

1

1. N, 2. M, 3. G, 4. A, 5. I, 6. B, 7. C, 8. F, 9. H, 10. E, 11. K, 12. D, 13. L (*central business district* is often abbreviated to *CBD*), 14. J

2

1. H, 2. B, 3. G, 4. F, 5. A, 6. C, 7. E, 8. D

3

1. metropolis, 2. cosmopolitan, 3. urban, 4. amenities, 5. cultural events, 6. infrastructure, 7. commuters, 8. central business district (CBD), 9. rush hour / peak periods, 10. congestion, 11. pollution, 12. cost of living, 13. building sites, 14. population explosion, 15. drug abuse, 16. inner-city, 17. rural, 18. prospects, 19. productive land / cultivation / arable land, 20. urban sprawl, 21. environment

Other words which you might find useful include:
development, employment, facilities, outskirts, property prices, residents, residential, suburbs, unemployment

Pages 100 – 101 Travel

1

1. False (a *travel agency*, sometimes called a *travel agent's*, is a place where you go to buy a holiday or ticket, and a *tour operator* is the company which sells the holiday to you via the travel agency)
2. True
3. True
4. False (they get *on*)
5. False (they get *off*)
6. True
7. True
8. True
9. True
10. False (*ecotourism* is supposed to be tourism that benefits or has a neutral effect on the environment, although this is not always the case)
11. False (they all have a slightly different meaning: use your dictionary to find out what these are)
12. False (it depends on the country you are from and where you are going. Citizens of the European Union, for example, do not need a visa if they are flying to another EU country)
13. False (it is a *short-haul* flight)
14. False (it is cheaper. We can say *tourist class* or *coach class* instead of economy class)
15. False (you only need to fill in an *immigration card* when you go to another country, but see number 12 above)
16. False (*cultural tourism* is a holiday taken in order to visit places that are culturally interesting, or to attend a cultural event. *Sustainable tourism* is tourism that causes minimal damage to the environment, similar to ecotourism)
17. True (We can also say *high season*. The opposite – the time of year when not many people take a holiday – is called the *low season* or *off season*)
18. False (a *cruise* is journey on a ship for pleasure, especially one that involves visiting a series of places. A holiday where you watch wild animals is called a *safari*)

Answers

19. False (an *armchair traveller* is someone who finds out what a place is like by watching travel programmes on television, reading travel books or looking at travel websites on the Internet)
20. True (we can use the adjective *touristy* to describe places like this)

2
1. refugees,   2. internally displaced,   3. emigration,   4. immigration,   5. culture shock,
6. expatriates (often informally shortened to *expats*),   7. UNHCR (the *United Nations High Commission for Refugees*),   8. deported,   9. persona non grata (a Latin phrase which describes a foreign person who is not allowed to visit or stay in another country),   10. economic migrants,
11. repatriated / deported,   12. border controls

3
1. travel agency,   2. package tour,   3. independent travellers,   4. visas,   5. check in (the place where you check in for a flight at an airport is called the *check-in desk / counter*),   6. economy class,
7. disembark,   8. mass tourism,   9. all-inclusive,   10. ecotourism,   11. refugees,   12. internally displaced,   13. economic migrants,   14. expatriates,   15. culture shock,   16. immigration,
17. persona non grata,   18. deported,   19. checking in,   20. excursion

Pages 102 – 104 Work

1
1. ☺,   2. ☹,   3. ☺,   4. ☺ (we also say *pay rise*),   5. ☹,   6. ☺,   7. ☹,   8. ☹,   9. ☹ (often abbreviated to *RSI*),   10. ☹,   11. ☺,   12. ☹,   13. ☺,   14. ☹,   15. ☺,   16. ☺,   17. ☺,   18. ☺,   19. ☹,   20. ☹,   21. ☹,
22. ☺ (we also say *incapacity benefit*),   23. ☹ (although some people enjoy having a demanding job),   24. ☺,   25 ☹   26 ☹

2
A. Tracy (E), B. Jane (A), C. Claire (B), D. Marie (F), E. Samantha (C), F. Jeanette (D)

3
1. employees,   2. unskilled,   3. semi-skilled,   4. blue collar,   5. manufacturing industries,   6. white-collar,   7. service industries,   8. job security,   9. steady job,   10. hiring,   11. firing,   12. stress,
13. demanding,   14. unsociable hours,   15. repetitive strain injury (RSI),   16. salary,   17. promotion,
18. perks,   19. incentive,   20. increment,   21. sickness benefit,   22. pension,   23. self-employed

Other words and phrases which you might find useful include:
candidate, dismiss, dismissal, employer, fixed income, interview, interviewee, interviewer, leave (= a formal word for a holiday from work: *She's on leave at the moment*), manual worker, overtime, profession, recruit, recruitment